Early Acclaim f

"Julia writes beautifully from her life's experience and journey. She speaks from her heart, asking insightful and penetrating questions with great clarity and perception. A book to stimulate your own spiritual path, inspiring transformation!"
—Michael H. Taylor, M.D., former Medical Editor for Yoga Journal

"The simple, yet powerful methods and inspiring stories in this book would be helpful for anyone on a spiritual path. I found the book fun to read, inspirational and very helpful."
—Jonathan Robinson, author of *The Complete Idiot's Guide to Awakening Your Spirituality* and *The Experience of God*

"This exceptional book translates the practice of jnana yoga, the yoga of wisdom, into a form which everyone can use. It guides the reader to probe deeply into the eternal questions that life presents to us humans—What is my truth? What's the lesson? What's necessary? Julia Tindall brings ancient wisdom to life in these pages in a form that is easily accessible and fun to read."
—Susan Campbell, Ph.D., author of *Getting Real: 10 Truth Skills You Need to Live an Authentic Life*

"Julia Tindall has led yoga classes at our ministry for a number of years with great success. Her very real commitment to developing our spiritual potentials, which has made her a successful teacher, is expressed so well in her book, *20 Questions for Enlightened Living.* It is a personal sharing that gives clear insight to guidelines for expanding one's life."
—Phillip Pierson, Senior Minister, Christ Unity Church, Co-host of "The Best is Yet to Be" TV show

"Julia Tindall has produced the perfect mix of practicality and inspiration. Her book helped me think in brand new ways about the challenges I face in life and gave me the practical steps I could take to out-distance my own blocks and make real progress."
—Bill Shireman, author of *What I Learned in the Rainforest*

20 Questions for Enlightened Living

peace and freedom through jnana yoga

Julia Tindall

First Edition

Printed in the United States of America

ISBN 0-9715894-5-3

Library of Congress Control Number: 2003111590

Heaven on Earth Project
PO Box 67
Mt Shasta CA 96067 USA

Phone/Fax: 530.918.9264

Email: info@hoep.org

Website: www.hoep.org

Dedicated to my teachers,

past, present, and future

Contents

Foreword .... **xiii**

INTRODUCTION **1**

What Is Jnana Yoga? **1**

Jnana Yoga in Our Everyday Lives **3**

The 10 Principal Aims of Jnana Yoga **4**

The Purpose of This Book **5**

How I Came to This Path **6**

How to Use This Book **7**

THE FOUNDATION **11**

1. How can I be grateful? **13**
Asking this question cultivates an attitude of acceptance and a heart full of joy

2. What's so? (What's going on right now?) **21**
Keeps us in the present moment

3. How does it feel? **29**
Gets us in touch with our authentic Self

4. What is my truth? **37**
Brings inner peace

THERE IS A MONSTER THAT EATS OUR PEACE **47**

5. What's the preference? **49**
Helps free us from disappointments

6. What's the desire? **55**
Aligns us with our true purpose

7. What's the judgment? **65**
Frees us from the rigidity of a fixed position

8. What's the criticism? **73**
Helps us relate to others

CLEARING UP THE PAST **83**

9. Who do I need to forgive? **85**
Heals our relationships and ourselves

10. Can I bring myself current? **93**
Releases us from the shackles of the past

11. What's the secret? **101**
Frees us from our shame

IN EACH MOMENT **109**

12. What would love do now? **111**
Transforms our relationships with ourselves and others

13. What's necessary? **119**
Conserves our energy

14. What's the hurry? **125**
Teaches patience, reduces stress

BREAKING OLD PATTERNS **133**

15. What's the lesson? **135**
Helps us to not repeat the same old behaviors

16. What's the melodrama? **141**
Diffuses our tendency to overreact

17. How do I know? **151**
Frees us from limiting belief systems

18. Who's in control? 159
Allows the flow of life to enter in

DANCING IN THE LIGHT 167

19. What makes my heart sing? 169
Puts us on our true path to bliss

20. How can I serve? 175
Brings us into alignment with God's Will

Afterword 181

The History of Jnana Yoga 183

Guidelines for Group Facilitation 189

Suggested Reading 195

Glossary of Terms 199

About the Author 201

Videotapes, Audiocassettes, and CDs 202

Seminars, Retreats, and Yoga Vacations 209

Acknowledgements

This book was inspired by my study of jnana yoga, the yoga of Self-inquiry. Many of the practices have come alive through the wealth of collective wisdom shared by my students and friends on retreats and classes throughout the years. In particular, I would like to thank Laura Hill for her ideas and encouragement, Yogi Baba for his unswerving love over the years, Ruth Pritchard for her faith in my ability, Kriyanandadevi, my yoga sister, and Pat Nielsen, wise-woman. For their inestimable help in the editing process I thank Eric Stryson and my father, Geoffrey Tindall. For their support of the jnana yoga process, I would like to thank my jnana yoga group members in Sacramento, many of whom have been the inspiration for tools, techniques, and examples shared in this book. For their faith in this book and their vision for the transformations this work can bring, I thank my publisher Aaron and his wife Bonnie. For their creative input with cover design I acknowledge my friends Armando Busick and Liberty McGeorge-Kester. Finally, I thank my mother, Doreen, for having me. She wishes you all to know that it hurt like hell at the time.

Foreword

There are many reasons why it is becoming imperative for each of us to seek a state of awakening within our own consciousness. As the energies in our world quicken and the pace of our life increases, just coping with the daily grind takes a great deal of balance. As the world shrinks into a global village, politics and the media deluge us with global issues, which come ever closer to home and challenge our hearts and minds to respond. In the apparent maelstrom of today's world, there is relief for us in gaining a larger vision of reality.

It is always important for people to be in synch with the times in which they live and to rise to the challenges they face, both as individuals and as communities. This is necessary in order for us to fulfill our evolutionary path. Our current times are asking a lot of us, and we cope best when we are able to stand in truth, integrity, and compassion and to draw from deeper and more real parts of ourselves. Life is forcing us through massive experiences of change, whether we like it or not, and for which, for the most part, our upbringing has not prepared us.

Whether we have formally signed up for transformation or not, it is happening. This is neither good nor bad, it is just what is. And under these circumstances, there are many advantages to and a great wisdom in deliberately engaging, with the most conscious intent, in the art of transformation. Doing this will give us the tools we need to help us cope with life—tools which assist us on the journey of understanding ourselves, of our place in life and in the day-to-day passage of time and events—tools for bringing our thoughts and feelings into a greater balance and compassion. In a world of constant change, the tools we seek are the timeless, changeless, universal principles of life and of Spirit.

One of these timeless teachings of universal truth is the practice of jnana yoga. In *20 Questions for Enlightened Living,*

Julia Tindall has chosen to focus on jnana yoga, the yoga of the mind, since the awakening of the mind leads us, very quickly, to begin opening to our inner freedom. She lays out a course of study that is simple to grasp, effective in practice, and that will stand us in good stead for many years of growth and transformation. And while jnana can sometimes seem to have an overly mental focus, Julia has structured her jnana method in a very user-friendly way with an all-encompassing whole-person and life-skills approach, making the teaching very understandable and practical.

Julia has done this with a fast and relevant approach to teaching the universal principles. She uses a format of asking questions which have the ability to penetrate into the heart of one's issues, and in finding the answers, the seeker is brought to a place of truth and self-revelation.

Form follows consciousness, and thus as we learn to change and shift our consciousness into states of balance and equanimity, we as a people will find the power to transform our lives and our outer world into something that fulfills our evolutionary needs—one person at a time. Julia's dynamic teachings can take us there.

Leslie Temple-Thurston
author of *Marriage of Spirit*

Introduction

What Is Jnana Yoga?

Have you ever felt that there must be something more to life, something beyond our mundane experience of the everyday world? From our childhood on we are programmed to conform to the reality we perceive around us, the reality that our family and friends perceive. We are conditioned to believe that we are only our personality, our thoughts. Yet, this is not so. The conditioned mind and structured personality are just a set of energies that overlay the original Self. So how do we discover the nature of this original Self?

Jnana yoga (pronounced nyah-nah) is a system of Self-inquiry whereby we gradually let go of our identification with the personality until the true Self is revealed. Just as hatha yoga stretches and opens the body, jnana yoga stretches and opens the mind. As we dissolve our description of reality, we realize the world is different than what we had imagined. Life becomes new, fresh. We become more discerning, more peaceful inside. Insights and clarity arise more readily and our lives become balanced and filled with Grace.

There are three main methods used in this Self-inquiry. The first is called "activating the witness consciousness." Our witness is our unbiased, neutral, eternal Self. It is who we really are. In order to cultivate our witness we consciously and deliberately examine how we feel, think, and behave. With this, we gradually strip away our layers of social conditioning and identification with the ego. We discover that the mind and awareness are not the same and that there is an intelligent part of us that can observe our mind dispassionately.

The second method is to ask the question "Who am I?" The approach used here is normally a stripping away of who we are not, which leads us to a place beyond the mind where nothing remains to describe the individual being but the true, essential nature of the Self. (For more on this see the Afterword).

The third technique involves bringing what has been unconscious into consciousness. It is important to uncover and dissolve the hidden patterns wedged in our unconscious in order to be free of them, as the newness and freshness constantly coming to us from Source is blocked by these patterns. Here we look at aspects of ourselves such as our unconscious behaviors, habits and addictions. We bring what has been in the dark into the light. It's as though we have to understand the functioning of this human system fully before we can move beyond it. We own all of our parts, and then we let them go.

As we progress in our practice of jnana yoga, we take a step back and observe ourselves on the stage of life, playing our role, like watching a movie on a screen. We are the actor, yet we also get to write our own script. Our witness is really our Divine Self watching the ego living life in this way. The more we strengthen our identification with our witness and the less with our egoic personality, the more we grow spiritually. As this process continues, we experience an emptying out, a letting go of our attachments, desires, fears, and stories. The more we empty, the greater our Presence and our love; the less we attach, the greater our delight and joy in the mystery of life; and the more we cultivate acceptance, the greater our contentment. We experience a "lightening up." Indeed, this is the process of achieving "en-lighten-ment."

The questions posed in this book present a format for this investigation of Self, as a method for identifying more fully with the witness and for understanding ourselves. Right from the start you the student will notice the possibility for experiencing life in a new, different way as the witness begins to activate. Even a little bit of jnana yoga practice goes a long way toward bringing more consciousness into daily life and along with it more clarity, peace and joy. The invitation here is to celebrate the process! How far down the road of awareness are you willing to tread?

> ***Yoga:*** *Sanskrit word meaning "union," specifically the union of self with God*
>
> ***Jnana Yoga:*** *The yoga of knowledge/Self-inquiry/ wisdom*
>
> ***Jnani:*** *One who practices jnana yoga*
>
> *Practicing jnana yoga brings clarity, higher awareness, and peace of mind. The jnani experiences the dissolving of all belief systems about himself as a separate being and all identification with ego, body, and mind until he becomes empty enough to merge his consciousness back into the oneness of Creation.*

Jnana Yoga in Our Everyday Lives

The great thing about jnana yoga is that we are constantly being offered opportunities to practice. It is very simple. It only requires that we are vigilant and pay attention. We are practicing jnana yoga when we:

- question why we work the jobs we do,
- ask ourselves why we fear what terrifies us,
- catch ourselves judging someone else or being critical with ourselves,
- examine the nature of our desires,
- elect to tell the truth rather than a lie because it doesn't feel good to lie,
- question our belief systems and discern what is true for us rather than believing what our parents or teachers taught us,
- observe an event in our lives that might normally have the power to disturb our peace, such as being the recipient of someone's anger, and remain neutral about it, and
- use our awareness to investigate our habitual patterns, and see why we do them.

The 10 Principal Aims of Jnana Yoga

These aims are the threads that run through this book.

1. To activate our witness consciousness, so we are at once the observer and the observed, noticing that when we shine the light of awareness on something it changes.
2. To cultivate a habit of gracious acceptance of life as it is rather than resisting the things we can't change.
3. To create freedom by letting go of our attachments to outcome and surrendering up our preferences to God.
4. To come fully into our feeling nature, so we can be more present with our experiences and move through our lessons more quickly.
5. To know that we are totally responsible for the quality of our experience of life and that how we respond in any situation is always our choice.
6. To realize that we can have no peace in the present without healing our past.
7. To appreciate the sacredness of life just as it is.
8. To feel what it is to be a person of integrity, speaking truth and being authentic.
9. To surrender our habit of control, so we can explore the frontiers of life's mysteries, rather than remaining in the safety of our known.
10. To realize that true joy is in living out our life's purpose as an instrument of God.

The Purpose of This Book

The purpose of this book is to provide an accessible entry point into the teachings of jnana yoga. The exercises presented here help us to practice being in witness consciousness so we can see the workings of our ego personality clearly for what they are. As we continue on this path we systematically work to let go of limiting belief systems that keep us stuck in old patterns, to heal our past, and to embrace all aspects of ourselves, until the unity and harmony we feel within can attract the oneness experience of Grace.

The tools offered in this book are experiential. They require our attention, commitment, and practice. If we use them, they have the power to change our lives in ways we may never have thought possible, helping us to break free of unconscious behaviors. The extent of the shift is up to us. How conscious can we be with the exercises? How willing are we to adopt new ways of relating to our world?

In the traditional psychotherapy approach, there is a tendency to see the patient as broken and in need of fixing. In jnana yoga, neither people nor situations are judged. Instead it is recognized that we are challenged in life. Yet in these challenges come our opportunities for growth and the chance to make choices from a place of higher awareness. We are all perfectly poised to learn our lessons. The question is, how much can we pay attention, to get the lesson sooner rather than later?

This book is the perfect guidebook for raising our awareness so we are capable of paying more attention. It offers the reader a series of open-ended questions to consider. These questions can help us with one of the greatest dilemmas we humans face—what goes on in our heads! For example, how do we stop our judgments from affecting our relationships with others? What do we do about our own inner critic that drives us crazy with self-recrimination? How do we handle it when we don't get what we want? It's all very well to be asked to forgive, but how do we know when we really have forgiven 100%? Jnana yoga offers tools to help with all this and more.

The questions are simple. Everyone can understand them. However, keeping the questions in consciousness in order to raise our awareness is a lifetime's practice. That is why this is a timeless book that can be read and re-read and worked and re-worked constantly throughout our lives. Life is always changing, and with each new circumstance the questions will again appear fresh and relevant to the reader.

Sometimes during the course of our lives we may get glimpses of unity consciousness, a so-called "enlightenment experience." But unless we have done the groundwork of jnana yoga, the chances are that we cannot hold the charge of staying in unity consciousness for very long, so the experience becomes a passing event rather than a true awakening. The more we use jnana yoga to clear ourselves of that which is illusory, and the less we identify with our ego-personality selves, the more we can hope to attract the enlightenment experience as a permanent state of being.

Signposts will appear along the way to tell us how we are doing with the practice. We can look at how well our life is working for us. For example, are we experiencing more inner tranquility? Are our relationships with others bringing us joy? There are no quick fixes in life, but there are always opportunities for more growth, more awareness, and ultimately more love. Are you ready for a fresh approach?

How I Came to This Path

I used to be a typical yuppie living it up in the City of London. A high-powered job in advertising took me to the fanciest restaurants, the flashiest press conferences, and the most exciting PR events. So how did an individual like myself, with a Type A personality and a B.A. in business, get to be hanging out in the woods with a yogi, spending time communing with nature and practicing yoga?

Well, I didn't come to the study of yoga easily. I came kicking and screaming, resisting the practices I was being taught with a will that reflected my independent streak. But at the time my yoga studies began, I was newly divorced and facing bankruptcy. I had felt terrorized by my ex-husband. A sense of powerlessness enveloped me. My situation had become unbearable, and finally I left town with just my cat and a few possessions. My life was a mess, my emotions were in tatters, and I knew I needed something to help me make sense of it all.

Yoga offered me a time-honored methodology to this end. As my studies progressed, I began to see the wisdom in the practices I was learning, and they in turn began to work for me. Now I had tools to help me deal with challenges as they arose. I had a hatha yoga practice to help balance my energies and emotions and keep me healthy. I had a jnana yoga practice to help ease the turbulence in my mind. Life got smoother—still intense, yet somehow more flowing—as I began to accept what showed up in my life instead of resisting what my ego-self told me I didn't like.

The awareness exercises presented here worked for me as baby steps towards embracing life the way it is. Now I'm sharing these exercises in this book, knowing that they will work for you, too.

How to Use This Book

Each chapter is in the form of a question. This is because the purpose of the teaching is not to give you pat answers to life's challenges but rather to invite Self-inquiry and raise awareness. Questions are useful here because they promote this investigation of Self in an open-ended and non-judgmental way and can serve as a reminder for us to constantly activate our witness consciousness. All chapters contain a purpose and a discussion on the question, followed by examples and exercises.

You may choose to spend one week practicing each exercise or longer. Do what feels right for you. However, I recommend a minimum of one week per chapter, in order to give your life an opportunity to come up with an issue that relates to the question. In my experience this tends to happen with incredible synchronicity. For example, if you are working with the question on melodrama, something dramatic may well occur to give you the chance to observe how you choose to respond.

You may also notice that the practice is cumulative; that is, we are never completely "done" with any of the questions but rather continue to progress in our experience of how our new awareness can help us along life's path. The more we work with the questions, the more they all fit together to help us gain in clarity and understanding.

The exercises can also be done jointly with friends. It's a great idea to set up a study group whereby you meet with a group of friends regularly and go through the book chapter by chapter. This way you can be each other's coach and confidant, encouraging each other along the way and sharing what insights and shifts come up for you all as you progress. (See Guidelines for Group Facilitation on pages 189–194.)

I suggest working with the chapters sequentially first. Then, once you've worked through the entire book, you can pick a chapter at random for each day or week and continue your exploration of the exercises.

This is a practice for the rest of your life. Have fun with it!

Tip: Write the question for the week on sticky notes and post them on the fridge and bathroom mirror as reminders, to constantly re-enforce the awareness!

Please note: In the book I often refer to "God." However, you may substitute whatever term that you are familiar with that refers to your relationship to the higher power, for example, "Creator," "Great Spirit," "Allah," "Jesus," "Divine Mother," or "Brahman."

THE FOUNDATION

Being grateful for what shows up in our lives, accepting *what's so,* feeling everything fully, and living our truth together form the core principles of jnana yoga. Simple as these principles are, our practice of them profoundly affects the quality of our life experience and helps to lay the foundation for the rest of the exercises presented in this book.

1

How can I be grateful?

Cultivates an attitude of acceptance and a heart full of joy

The practice of gratitude is a great place to start our spiritual journey, as it is simple to do, yet has incredible power to change our lives. Indeed, it is the practice I fall back on the most if I feel down or depressed. It changes my mood quickly and profoundly and puts life's events in their proper perspective.

Form follows consciousness, so we attract what we focus on. If we focus on lack and complain about what we don't have and how terrible life is, we will create more of the lack. However, if we can find it in our hearts to be grateful for what we have, our experience becomes one of joyful abundance, no matter what our actual circumstance.

The children are our teachers...

This has been so clearly illustrated for me when I have spent time in third world countries. I became friends with a simple family in Burma who saw everything in their lives as a blessing: each meal they ate, all visitors to their humble abode—everything. They were grateful for every part of their lives. Their nine-year-old son sold chewing gum to the tourists to earn a little extra cash for the family. On the day I was leaving, he ran up to me with joy and offered me the only thing he had to give—a piece of chewing gum. I felt so blessed by his natural kindness. It touched my heart more than anything ever had.

To see little children in poorer nations playing with delight with makeshift toys, I am always struck by how attitude is everything and how those who have less are often grateful for more. One time I was visiting a tiny island called Lamu off the east Kenya coast and went for a walk through a small village there. I came across some children playing "cricket" with pieces of wood for bats and a rolled-up newspaper for a ball. I happened to have brought with me some gifts to give away and one of the things I had with me that day was an old tennis ball. I will never forget the gratitude in those children's eyes when they saw that the ball was for them. It brought tears to my eyes to see their joy over something so simple.

Another example a little closer to home is that of a friend of mine who was feeling depressed one day and saw a homeless person while out shopping. He thought, "At least I'm not as bad off as that person." Then as he got closer to the bag lady, he heard her singing joyfully. He thought, "Oh—I'm not as well off as this person!" This experience really got him to stop and think about his own attitude to gratitude.

Gratitude vs. desire…

In the western world we are inundated with advertisements whose job is to create desire in us, the consumer, so we will trot out and buy the advertised products. Because all of our desires can rarely be fulfilled, we are often left with a feeling that we don't have enough. We may fulfill one desire but after that there is another waiting to take its place. And another, and another. The cup of desire is bottomless.

Our challenge here is to disconnect from that artificial pressure, to be grateful instead for what we do have rather than be envious of what we have not. In this way gratitude can help us to seal the bottom of our cup of endless desire.

So often people pray to God to fulfill their desires. This kind of prayer affirms to the universe that we are discontented with what we have. It can sound a little whiny! Instead, we can offer God prayers of thanks for what we do have. Practicing this also helps us to stay in present time rather than projecting into the future with wishes and dreams. If we are always thinking that we'll only be happy when we have that product, the right mate, the perfect job, then we can never really be content and at peace with our current reality. Now is all we have and the more we stay conscious and present with our Now and are grateful for it, the greater our chances of happiness and peace.

Gratitude for our pain...

It is easier to be grateful for the good things in life, and this is a great way to begin a practice of gratitude. Then we can begin to look at our more challenging situations and start to find some gratitude for them, too. One of my teachers would always start our yoga classes with a prayer thanking God for the tests and challenges of daily life. After all, wouldn't life be dull without them? Being tested and stretched by life's events helps us to grow into our full potential. Without knowing sadness, how can we know joy? Without loneliness, how can we know union? And without fear, how can we know love? The magical thing is that when we take the step of embracing our pain, it transforms the nature of our experience into something more manageable, more meaningful. This gives us a great illustration of how our life experience depends on how we choose to respond to situations rather than on the situation itself. We are always at choice.

If being grateful for our pain is hard, rather than asking God to change our life circumstances we can ask God for help in perceiving things differently. For example, we can ask to see the golden lining in every situation. This is not always immediately clear, especially if we have our heart set on one thing and then something completely different shows up! But in my experience, what happens to us in life always has some benefit if we can only accept it and see it.

Our inspiration for this is surely Christopher Reeve, the handsome actor who became a quadriplegic in a horse-riding accident. Despite losing the use of his body, he has not lost his optimism and zest for life. Christopher is using his changed circumstances to inspire others to gratitude, no matter what their situation, and to encourage them to move forward on their healing journey. With Christopher as our example, we can see how it is possible to be in a place of offering God prayers of gratitude for everything that occurs, helping us respond positively to all situations.

The practice of gratitude is not, however, a denial of life's difficulties. Rather, it is a potential antidote to feelings of scarcity, negativity, and loss. We can choose to meet each moment as it arises with an open, joyous heart, instead of dwelling on negative feelings of dissatisfaction. Nor is it an excuse to become passive, hopeless, or helpless in the face of injustices or personal problems. We can accept what is and be grateful for the opportunity to grow and change in the light of our circumstances while still taking action in ways that are appropriate.

Our gratitude ratio...

As part of our Self-inquiry we can notice how much we focus on lack and complaints rather than on appreciation and gratitude. Some of us are walking emotional time-bombs, allowing simple, often meaningless events to set us off in explosions of anger, frustration, and complaint. If this is our everyday reality and much of our time is spent indulging in these negative reactions, the chances are we are pretty miserable people to be around. We are making our life harder than it needs to be! Practicing gratitude and appreciation throughout the day can change this. It can shift our mental and emotional state into one of peace and generosity, helping us to experience more joy and pleasure in our lives.

The more we train our minds in gratitude, the more our minds can stay attuned to experiencing greater joy when wonderful things happen to us! For example, when we take the first few bites of a fantastic food, we savor the delight of the taste. But after a while the taste-buds get used to the flavor and the mind is no longer as delighted. When we cultivate more appreciation, we can stay conscious of great taste right up until the last bite!

Gratitude as ownership...

There are often parts of ourselves that we push away and prefer to ignore, our shadow side, our evil twin who wants to be bitchy, sarcastic, critical, and angry. But these personality traits are also part of us, and when we deny them we deny a part of ourselves. Instead of denial, being grateful for these parts of us helps us to own them and to be more real and authentic with ourselves. After all, these character traits can also serve us. For example, our inner critic can make us judgmental, but also helps us to be discerning. With awareness, we can make this trait our servant rather than our master.

Gratitude for our shadow side enables us be more aware of the workings of our mind and helps us watch ourselves as we think our thoughts. We might say to ourselves, "Thank you for the opinion I didn't ask for." Or, "Thank you for my ingratitude!" In this way we embrace all of our humanness in an accepting way that gives us a more peaceful presence in our lives rather than resisting who it is we are.

Gratitude for the Creation...

The yogis say that a human life is a precious thing indeed. It gives us the opportunity to experience all aspects of the creation, from the joys to the sorrows. There is therefore **nothing** not to be grateful for. Embrace all of it! Surrendering and being grateful for what life presents us with is the best way to acknowledge the Creation just the way it is and move into a place of acceptance and peace with our world. It cultivates a feeling of being blessed, a way to appreciate the miracle of life, rather than remaining focused on what is lacking. To sum up, practicing gratitude is the best way to feel rich, to express our love of God, and by far the best way to pray.

Get an attitude of gratitude!

Examples:

I have been leading yoga vacations in Mexico for the last few years. We go to out-of-the-way, indigenous places in order to experience the charm and culture of small Mexican villages. I always warn the groups that things there will not be quite like they are at home. The cockerels may wake us up at four o'clock in the morning, the plumbing is delicate and toilets do overflow, sometimes the water gets turned off for mysterious reasons, and there are dangerous and scary-looking insects lurking in dark corners. In order to help the group adjust, I now invite them to do a practice of gratitude as soon as we arrive, so instead of complaining about what's not up to American standards they can focus instead on the opportunity to expand out of their known horizons and into a new experience. This last year in the Yucatan, a lady in our group went back to her hut after dinner to find an enormous tarantula pasted onto her front door! Instead of being distressed, she ran back to the restaurant excitedly and invited all of us to come and look at her "visitor!"

A friend of mine broke his leg. He watched how people around him sympathized with his misfortune and held him in their consciousness as a victim of circumstance. However, this was not his experience. He was grateful for the broken leg. It gave him an opportunity to slow down from his busy schedule. He was also forced into a position where he had to receive from others—something that was hard for him. So he embraced the broken leg with joy and gratitude, knowing that it was a place of learning and opportunity for him. In this place he certainly did not feel like a victim!

A girlfriend of mine had a hard time growing up in a controlling family and left home as soon as she could. She now sees clearly the pain and melodrama in her parents' lives. They did not know how to live a life filled with joy and bliss, so in their own way they encouraged her to go out and find it on her own. She did. Now she can be grateful about her childhood, as she sees how her parents helped to shape who she is today! She sees their pain, that they could not do anything else, and that it wasn't personal. Any daughter or son of theirs would have received the same treatment. They did the best that they could at the time. She carries no blame or remorse for her upbringing and instead only feels gratitude and love. As a result, she now has a much better relationship with her parents.

My friend Laura changed jobs and was faced with a 45-minute commute each way to work. At first she was dismayed at the amount of time she was spending in her car. But then she was grateful for the commute, as it gave her the opportunity to sing, listen to books on tape, and even learn Spanish!

There have been periods of time in my life when I have been alone, without a romantic partner. My mind has often complained about this and it has been hard for me to feel grateful for the loneliness. However, with the benefit of hindsight I have seen that those periods of alone-time were important for my personal growth and development. They helped me connect with my inner core and get in touch with my life's purpose without the distraction of relationship. Now I know that if ever these alone periods should show up, I can choose to celebrate them! I get to do exactly as I please and live the way I choose. Besides, everything always changes! So being grateful for the alone-time when it occurs helps me to get the most value from it.

> *"I have accepted the way I am, and that very moment all problems disappeared, that very moment all worries disappeared. Not that I became perfect, but I started enjoying my imperfections."*
> —Osho, *The Tantra Experience*

Exercises:

Immediate action:

Enlist the help of your witness to transform complaint and dissatisfaction into appreciation. Every time you hear yourself complain about something, follow it with a statement of gratitude, either out loud or silently to yourself. For example:

"I had to park far away from the store and now I have to walk a long way for my groceries—but I'm grateful for my strong legs and the exercise I'm getting with this walk."

"The roof of my house is leaking and I will have to replace it—but I'm really grateful that I have a home of my own."

Ongoing awareness:

This exercise can be done anytime, anywhere, but I strongly

suggest practicing it in the early morning and last thing at night.

When you wake up in the morning, immediately start to give thanks for all the things in your life. Start with the obvious blessings, such as your health, the companionship of friends and animals, the warmth of your bed, the love of your family, the opportunity to be alive for one more day...and then move on to be grateful for the challenges you are facing. Just spend a few moments offering up these thoughts to God. Notice what comes up for you as you do this.

Do the same as soon as you get into bed ready for sleep at night.

Eventually you can get into the spirit of gratitude continually. Thank God for anything and everything. In this way, you can make each moment sacred and feel gratitude for the abundance of life, feeling connected with the gifts you have been given. Make "Thank you" your mantra and say "Yes" to life!

It was the middle of winter and a saint was traveling in India with his entourage. They had no warm clothes and nowhere to sleep. The saint sat under a tree and began to give thanks to Divine Mother. A disciple asked, "Master, we are tired, cold, and hungry, and you are giving thanks to Divine Mother. Why are you doing this?"

The Saint replied, "You don't understand—Divine Mother wants us to experience poverty and that's just what we need right now. So I'm giving thanks for the experience and celebrating the poverty!"

2

What's so? (What's going on right now?)

Keeps us in the present moment

"What's so?" refers to whatever is actually going on in the present moment. We can experience *what's so* most clearly by the technique I refer to as "activating our witness consciousness." Imagine we can take a step outside of ourselves and observe everything around us as though seeing it on a movie screen. We watch our environment, the people around us, what we ourselves are experiencing—everything about our current reality. We observe as objectively as we can, without the mind's interpretations.

For example: I am sitting in the car stuck in traffic, late for an appointment. I start to worry that my friend will be upset that I am late and will not wait for me. My mind conjectures all the possible scenarios that may occur and I get frustrated, even angry about the traffic not moving. Then my witness consciousness kicks in. I watch my mind spinning off into the future with worry and I observe my emotional state and the tension it has caused in my body. I bring myself present and see that the traffic jam is just *"what is so."* There is nothing I can do about it but I do have a choice in how I respond. In the light of this self-observation my emotions calm down and I stop worrying. Instead I begin to breathe deeply and look at the beautiful trees by the road.

Interestingly enough, quantum physics has come to the same conclusion—that whatever we observe is affected by our observation, and changes! So just this simple act of activating our witness consciousness can change our experience of life profoundly. The more we observe ourselves, the greater our capacity to change our emotional state and perceptions so we can see things in a more accepting, loving way.

Honing our skills...

To truly experience *what's so* we must get real and separate the facts from our ideas about the facts. We must set aside beliefs about what we think should or shouldn't happen, what we expect to happen, or what we consider acceptable. These beliefs are our training. They may come from parents, school, church, or society. They color our perceptions and lead to denial, resistance, and a suppression of our true feelings, as opposed to an authentic acceptance of *what's so*. Wearing rose-colored glasses around our loved ones is a good example of this. When we fall in love we hold that person in the highest light and tend to see only their best qualities. This perception clouds our judgment.

I have a friend whose husband cheated on her for many months. He would disappear for hours at a time. She saw lipstick on his collar, credit card bills reflecting hotel charges she knew nothing about, and other such evidence. Still, she did not want to confront her husband about this and held on tightly to the belief that she had a wonderful marriage and all was well. She refused to believe that her husband would lie to her and chose instead to be in total denial of his behavior. One day, however, he finally confessed to the adultery and told her he was leaving. At that point my friend's suppressed feelings of anger and grief came out and she was forced into accepting not only the situation but also her own pain.

In my friend's case, resistance to what was so led to a much harder blow to her life when the truth finally came out. If she had confronted her husband earlier, it is possible they could have gone to a counselor with their problems and saved their marriage. Any strategies or manipulations we enlist to help us avoid a full experience of our lives have a tendency to backfire on us. If God is asking us to experience something and we resist, the only alternative for God is to keep making the experience bigger until we can no longer avoid it. Better to be vigilant about *what's so* and be available for our experiences in their gentlest form rather than a more painful alternative.

Practicing this pure observation also frees us from our tendency to make assumptions and interpret what we think is happening. For example, I was leading a weekend retreat and one of the participants was very withdrawn from the group and did not join us in all the activities. She was very quiet and spent a lot of time alone. That was what I observed. My mind wanted to interpret her behavior. I could have imagined she was not having a good time or that she didn't like what I was doing. If I had allowed my mind to go there I would have been making what turned out to be a false assumption. My interpretation was not what was so. Instead, I asked her how she was doing. She told me that a friend of hers had just passed away and that she was really grateful for this weekend to feel supported in her grieving and the permission I gave her to participate only when she wanted to. It was the perfect scenario for her and she was doing just fine.

Freeing us from worry...

My grandmother was a worrier. My mother worries. I inherited from them a predisposition to worry about the details of my life. Will I be on time for the plane? Will my boyfriend remember it was my birthday? Am I going to get sick before I have to teach a workshop? I used to waste a whole lot of time being overly concerned about nonexistent future events. Asking *"What's so?"* has been a great tool in helping to shift this habit for me as it invites us to look only at what's going on in the present moment and not speculate about what might happen in the future. Am I OK now? And now?

Worry is a waste of our precious energy. It holds our mind in future time, feeding our fear and taking us out of experiencing the fullness of the present moment. It does nothing to change our situation but it does disturb our peace of mind. What we focus on expands, so when we worry, we run the risk of attracting to us the very thing that we fear. Far better to do as Bobby McFerrin's song says, "Don't worry, be happy!"

Worry is praying for what we don't want...

Releasing regret and remorse...

Asking *"What's so?"* also helps us release feelings of regretting the past and wallowing in self-pity and self-scrutiny. Thoughts of "if only" or dreams of "what could have been" entrench us squarely in the position of victim, making us feel like we are stuck in an unacceptable present. These thoughts do not serve us! Like worrying about the future, they steal our precious energy. We are at choice in how we perceive our lives. We can commiserate and complain about how unfair life is or we can accept that this is *what's so* and ask how we can learn and grow from the situation rather than resisting it.

A close friend of mine had a 10-year-long affair with a married man who kept promising her he would leave his wife and be with her forever. The day never came. However, my friend waited and waited for this man to become available.

Eventually she found out that this man was a liar. He had even had another affair during that time and had told the other lady the same things! My friend ended the relationship. She could have been very bitter and languished in a space of regret and remorse over those wasted years of waiting for what was never to transpire. Instead, she got over it. She took up golf, singing, and traveling. She decided to be more discerning next time around and only date men who were available!

Appropriate action...

There is no need for resignation or apathy. In any situation, we can ask ourselves if there is an appropriate action necessary or possible to take and if there is, do it. Here's an example. My friend Chris used to drive an old Volkswagen Bug. The brakes did not work well and he used to worry he would get into an accident and even had dreams of pressing the brake pedal and having no response! He would feel sorry for himself that he did not have the money to buy a newer car. However, in this case there was clearly action he could take to remedy the source of his worry. He ended his procrastination, took the car in and got the brakes fixed.

After we've done whatever action is necessary or possible to change our situation, all that remains is to surrender up the outcome to Divine Will and accept whatever happens next. So the process is:

1. Observe *what is so*.
2. Ask ourselves if there is anything we need to change or can change about the situation.
3. If so, do it.
4. Accept the outcome.

Eating the fear...

When we raise our consciousness to ask the question *"What's so?"* it changes the nature of our fear from being our master to being our servant. Either what we are afraid of has not yet happened, in which case, why worry? Or, it has happened and we are busy dealing with the consequences and probably too occupied to be afraid. In both cases there's no more room for fear.

In Summary...

Asking *"What's so?"* helps us to be at peace with the way it is in the world, to accept life just as it shows up for us. It invites us to slow down for a moment and take a look at what's happening now. We get to deal with what is right in front of us instead of speculating on a nonexistent future or complaining about a past that cannot be changed. This whole process helps us to feel grounded and centered and more at ease with our life, with the added benefit of enhancing the richness of our experience of the present moment.

> *"Our greatest adversaries are the past and the future. Both are robbers of the precious moment."*
> —Pat Nielsen, wise woman

Examples:

One summer's day my friend invited me to go for a drive to the mountains in his Porsche. We decided to go and hike to a lake that we'd never been to before. On the way, the road turned into a one-lane dirt track. It became steeper and steeper and rockier and rockier, with huge drop-offs on either side of the road! My friend began to get concerned. He explained to me that Porsches are not meant for this kind of driving. He wasn't sure if we would make it to the top.

Picking up on my friend's concern, I started to worry too. Then I caught myself. I asked, *"What's so?"* and *what was so* was that the car was still running right along and we had not yet fallen down the cliff. And besides, there was nothing I could do about the car's mechanics. I stopped worrying and relaxed. We made it just fine.

A friend of mine has an elderly aunt who was taken to the hospital recently with some health problems. As the closest relative, my friend had to deal with all the responsibility and worry of the situation. She used the question "What's so?" *to help her stay calm instead of over-dramatizing the situation. Yes, her aunt was being well cared for. She was alive. Everything that could be done was being done. It was OK. There was nothing lacking. Her aunt's health challenge was just* what was so.

A few years ago I was leading a yoga retreat at Mount Shasta in the summertime. This was a camping trip and we were all sleeping outside in tents and doing our yoga practice under the trees in the mornings with the beautiful blue sky above us. One day the clouds started to gather in the late afternoon. By evening the rain had begun—and so had the machinations of my mind as I wondered where I was going to be able to lead a yoga practice the next day if the ground was wet! It rained all night and the next morning we woke up to yet more rain. I watched myself worry about my students.

Then witness consciousness kicked in. There was nothing I could do about the rain, but I could remain optimistic and cheerful and be a little creative in our yoga practice!

I talked to the lady who ran the campsite and asked for her advice. She pointed me to the games room. Kindly, she offered to turn off the video machines and said we could at least gather in there by the pool table. Armed with an inspiration, I woke my students and invited them up to the games room. We proceeded to do a ledge series for opening the hips, with everyone putting one of their legs up on the pool table! We really made the best of it and had a great and humorous practice that no one will ever forget!

Serenity Prayer

Lord, grant me the serenity
to accept the things I cannot change,
The courage to change the things I can,
And the wisdom to know the difference.

Exercises:

Specific exercise:

Just for a day, watch when your mind races into the future and starts to conjecture with "What ifs?" Notice the fear of uncertainty that comes up and instead bring yourself present with what's going on right now.

Ongoing awareness:

When you catch yourself worrying, ask yourself, "What's so in this moment?" Then go through the procedure: observe, take action if necessary or possible, accept the outcome.

There once was a small fishing village many years ago where a young girl got pregnant by a sailor without being married. She delivered a baby boy but knew she could not keep the child or the village would ostracize her.

Up on the hill there lived a monk. The girl spread the story in the village that it was the monk who had fathered her child. One day the young girl climbed the hill and knocked on the door of the house where the monk lived. The monk answered the door and the girl presented him with the baby boy, saying that the child was his and he should take care of him. Without a word the monk took the baby and the girl departed.

Seven years went by. The boy grew up happily, with the monk looking after him. Then one day, the sailor returned and married the girl. She started to think about the son she had given up and decided that she wanted him back. So she climbed the hill once more and knocked on the monk's door.

"I've come for my boy," she said. "He's mine, not yours."

Without a word, the monk fetched the boy, gave him to the girl and shut the door. The girl left with her son and the monk went back to his meditation. Nothing was outside of his practice. It was all what was so.

3

How does it feel?

Gets us in touch with our authentic Self

I was raised in the king of all dispassionate countries—England! As a child I remember my grandmother's concerns about "what the neighbors might see" and how any serious talking would be done behind closed doors to maintain appearances for the world at large. This may sound Victorian, but believe me, most of the society I grew up in held the same attitude. We were taught to stifle our emotions and feelings, not express them. "Big boys don't cry," "stiff upper lip," and all that.

I don't think I cried until I was in my thirties and had moved to America. By that time I was so out of touch with my feelings that I had no idea I had any at all. I was ruled by my head and my keen intellect, never my heart or my sense of intuition. It has taken many years of diligent inward searching to shift that for myself. Even now I am challenged by my inclination to hold my true feelings back just to please others, instead of speaking my truth.

Although attitudes seem much looser in America, here, too, I have noticed that many people shy away from being aware of their feelings and expressing them in a healthy way. Numbing out with drugs and alcohol, or distracting with workaholism and shopping, is common everywhere.

Most of us start this numbing out process as little children. If we are sensitive and have landed in family situations that don't feel safe for us, we stop feeling because it hurts too much. Instead, we develop coping mechanisms that allow us to switch off from the pain of our emotions. Some of us retreat to the safety of our heads. We develop the intellect and our capacity for linear thinking. Not bad things, in and of themselves, but without our feeling nature to balance them this can lead to a life void of sensitivity and warmth, far removed from the true nature of our being.

Witnessing our emotions...

There is a difference between emotions and feelings. Whilst feelings are more connected to our witness state, emotions belong to the personality. They are part of our humanness and often trigger us into reactions where we "lash out' in anger or "crumple up" in grief. When these emotions arise, we tend to identify with them. We say " I am happy," "I am angry" etc. Our language reflects this identification with these transitory states. However, we are expressing something that is, on deeper analysis, not true. Instead, we can use our witness to take a step back, notice what is happening, feel the emotions fully and think, "I am aware of anger passing through me." Or, "Right now I'm noticing my heart is bursting with joy."

This does not mean we deny our emotions or stuff them. We feel them fully, yet observe ourselves feeling them from the vantage point of the witness which gives rise to a completely different experience of the situation. We could say that adding the component of our witness transforms the drama of emotions into the experience of feelings. We are no longer at the mercy of unbridled emotion. There is just *"what's so"* in the moment.

> *"Don't think, feel.*
> *Or you will miss all that heavenly glory."*
> —from Enter the Dragon, a Bruce Lee movie

Feelings as guideposts for clear perception...

Feelings occur when we perceive the subtle vibrations of the creation, which are actually passing through us all the time. They are associated more with our observer/witness state. As we proceed along our spiritual path and start clearing out the layers of our ego/personality, we become more sensitive. Our bodies become like tuning forks for these vibrations of existence and we start to perceive more clearly. We are more able to appreciate great art or music, more able to enjoy the richness of life.

As we get more in touch with these subtle feelings we may notice that things that pleased us before may no longer do so. Our dietary habits may change. We may no longer wish to hang out with the biker boys at the bar or watch violent movies. In other words increased sensitivity leads to naturally occurring life changes.

As we become more sensitive we are more able to discern the voice of God speaking to us. This is very helpful. The yogis say that God speaks to us through our feelings and our intuition (gut feeling), so feelings help us to be true to ourselves. My experience is that when I am able to get quiet enough to check inside with how something feels and I act on this instinct, life runs much more smoothly. Ultimately all answers and guidance come from within, so checking in with our feelings is a useful habit to cultivate.

When emotions and feelings are unexpressed...

When something upsets us, if we are aware of our feelings about it, we can deal with it and move through it. But if we are not consciously aware of how something is affecting us, our bodies certainly are and will contract and store that memory in our cells. When we don't allow our emotions a way to express, we end up storing them in our bodies until we are ready to dig them out and release them. So it is better to be aware of our emotions in the moment than to have to deal with a "pain in the neck" or a sore elbow down the line.

For example, a hurt heart full of sorrow will produce "armoring," hard, contracted muscles around the chest and shoulder areas, which feel tight and dense to the touch. We can lie to ourselves but the body does not lie to us. I first learned about this at massage school. When we touch a person in those places where the emotion is stored very often the person will re-experience those same emotions as they release them out again through the massage. When the emotions have been released there is a definite change in the quality of the tissue—it feels softer, squishier and more yielding to the touch. Hatha Yoga is another way to access this information. As we explore the yoga postures it soon becomes clear where our bodies are restricted and we often experience emotional release as the restricted places release and soften.

Many of us have suppressed our feeling nature for so long that it can take a while to surface again. We have often developed strategies for not allowing ourselves to feel or emote fully, like addictions to food, shopping, alcohol, even advice-giving! The first step is to become aware of these behaviors and notice what happens when we cut them out. Very often when we change our patterns in this way, the uncomfortable emotions that we have tried to suppress will bubble up and we will get another opportunity to feel them fully. Like any spiritual practice this takes courage, commitment and patience. The great thing is that we have constant opportunity to practice! After all, there's always something going on to feel!

> *"A yogi experiences anger fully—but just for a moment, and then lets it go."*
> —Babahaladarananda

With others...

Our relationships with others can be greatly enhanced if we practice expressing our feelings clearly as they arise. When we say, "I feel such and such.." it becomes a truth for us that no one else can deny. It's *"what's so"* for us—without blame or judgment. It is simply our truth. When we get skilled at this, our partners and friends always know where they stand with us. Nothing is withheld. There is clarity, honesty and clear communication in the moment. In this place, there can be greater trust, safety and love in our relationships.

I have four planets in Libra in my astrology chart—which gives me a predisposition to be "nice" at the cost of denying myself. We Librans are known as charming social butterflies and hurting other people's feelings is something that we abhor! In learning to express my feelings with others I have had to overcome this "nice" tendency. I have come to learn that my feelings are valid and it is ok to tell others how I feel, even though it may not be what they want to hear! (more on this in the next chapter).

Expanding the senses...

The other aspect of feeling is to experience as fully as possible through the senses, adopting a Zen-style approach to being as aware as possible of all stimulation to our senses of sight, smell, taste, touch and hearing. This takes some practice, but can eventually expand our consciousness, bring us into the present moment and gift us with new experiences in quite unexpected ways. Practicing the "awareness moment" in the exercises below is very helpful in developing this capacity.

During one period of intense yogic study, I would do a sense awareness exercise to connect with Nature twice a week. One day after taking a walk in the country and doing this practice, I heard a sound on the road behind me. When I looked round, I saw a deer trotting down the road, intent on following me. I stood still and the deer approached. It came up and nuzzled me. I stayed and petted the deer for at least 20 minutes, marveling at why this should be happening. It had no fear of me. My teacher said it was because it sensed my connectedness with Nature, which comes from this practice of expanding consciousness through the senses (see Nature Exercise below).

Why we are here...

I believe we are here on the planet to experience as much as possible. We can't do that if our feelings are shut down. So let's do God a favor and work on opening ourselves back up to our feeling nature so we can really play out our roles here with gusto!

Examples:

My partner has noticed my tendency to hide away in silence when I'm upset about something. When I do this, his greatest gift to me is to ask me what's going on and encourage me to share my thoughts and feelings, instead of holding everything inside. When I do, we feel much closer, more intimate and open.

Once I had my heart broken really badly. I was in agony, obsessed, overwhelmed with grief and completely dysfunctional. I sank into a sorrowful depression for the first time in my life. Nothing mattered any more. I didn't even want to get up in the morning. I could have chosen to distract myself from these feelings by going out to see friends or going to the movies. Instead, I chose to just feel the pain of it, experiencing my grief fully, until one day I was all cried out and the sorrow left me as quickly as it had come. I felt fine again and ready to continue with life, having released my attachment to the old relationship.

I have a friend who always makes fun of me. It's his way of being cute and it's often very funny, but at my expense. For the longest time I told myself he only did this because he liked me and it didn't matter. I numbed myself out completely around this, but noticed that I often had a minor stomachache when I was out with him. Finally with a bit of practice at feeling my feelings, I realized that it hurt when he made fun of me. I told him so and he has since stopped. My stomachache has cleared up, too.

Exercises:

Immediate action:

Take an "awareness moment" a few times each day. Stop—and check in with yourself and see how you are feeling. Feel your emotions, feel what's going on with your physical body and be aware of your surroundings—feel the texture of the car seat, smell the air, hear the birds sing, taste your food, see the beauty of Nature. Take this moment to honor your experience of life as fully as possible.

Nature Exercise: Go out to a quiet spot in Nature. See the sky, hear the sky, taste the sky, smell the sky and touch the sky. Lower your eyes and do the same with a distant tree. Then a closer tree. Finally, a bush and then the grass around you. Let go of the mind here and let yourself have an experience beyond your known.

Ongoing awareness:

Look to see where in your life you are hiding your feelings and emotions and when you have a tendency to numb yourself from them. Examine your strategies for numbing out, like eating, shopping, workaholism. Uncover your feelings, own them, speak about them. Give them a voice. Notice what happens.

Start to notice how it feels to wake up to being in witness, even during intense emotional times. Which areas of life is it harder to stay in witness? Maybe in relationships, dealing with money, children, traffic or work. As you notice that, begin the practice of staying in witness as much as possible in these more challenging situations too.

Charlotte Selver, teacher of sensory awareness, was leading a workshop at Esalen Institute in Big Sur, California. She placed a bowl of shelled almonds in the center of the group and offered one to everyone. Some grabbed an almond and ate it immediately. Others held onto it a while, then nibbled slowly.

Then Charlotte offered everyone another almond. This time she invited the group not to eat it straight away. "Can you feel the weight of the almond in your hand?" Charlotte asked. "How close must you bring it to your nose to be able to smell it?" Saliva was already flowing! Finally, "Try the almond—but notice what happens to it after it enters your mouth! How long can you taste it?"

No-one had suspected that an activity we had repeated so many thousands of times contained such a possibility of new experience. Charlotte had found a way to bring consciousness to what, next to breathing, is the most everyday of all activities, yet at the same time a central mystery; the passage of life from one form to another.

—Adapted from *Sensory Awareness,* by Charles Brooks

4

What is my truth?

Brings inner peace

Getting in touch with our truth so we can be in integrity is a crucial part of self-awareness. It's about *"what's so"* for us, how we feel, what is in our heart, our mind, our emotions at any given time. Our truth is ours alone. It doesn't belong to anyone else, nor can anyone tell us our truth is not so. It is our experience, and as such is undeniable.

Getting in touch with our truth so we can be in integrity is a crucial part of self-awareness. It's about *"what's so"* for us, how we feel, what is in our heart, our mind, our emotions at any given time. Our truth is ours alone. It doesn't belong to anyone else, nor can anyone tell us our truth is not so. It is our experience, and as such is undeniable.

When we are babies we express our truth freely. We cry when we are hungry, smile and coo when we are happy, and scream when something hurts. But as we grow older things happen to change that. We are told, "Be brave" and "Don't whine." Sometimes we are chastised for speaking out, punished in some way, and it becomes no longer safe to speak our truth. Instead we learn to conform and to please our parents and other adults. Gradually that inability to express ourselves truthfully is lost as we don the masks of civilized society to the point where as adults many of us have lost the ability to even feel at all what our truth is. We go along with the crowd so as not to rock the boat. We learn to please others before ourselves, and we think that this will keep us safe and happy.

Well, it won't. At least, not in the long term. The price we pay for suppressed truth is a huge loss of self-worth. If we cannot be responsible to ourselves first and foremost, we will tend to attract people into our lives who take advantage of this and use and abuse us in some way. This is the pattern of the typical co-dependents who value themselves for what they think they are doing to help others rather than valuing themselves for who they intrinsically are. This type of person is lost. The typical "people-pleasers," it's as though there's nobody real inside of them anymore.

I know about this place because this description fit me for so many years. Too afraid to speak up for myself, I talked in superficialities and knew how to play the part of the charming hostess very well. I was "nice." But inside I knew something was wrong, deeply wrong. My husband would put me down in public and emotionally abuse me so frequently that I stopped even noticing. He pushed me into doing things that I knew were wrong, but I went along with the program to protect my marriage (I thought) and continue my life-style, until I could stand it no longer.

At that time, without the tools of the yoga to help me, all I knew was to run away and get out of my situation. It took me years of careful work to rebuild the tatters of my frayed emotions and see clearly how being unable to speak my truth had caused my life to fall down around me like a pack of cards. What a lesson! Now I can be grateful for the whole experience and all it taught me. I can look for the red flags of my own co-dependence sooner rather than later, and if I become aware that I am not speaking up for myself, I now feel empowered to change that pattern. As a result I now have healthy relationships where I express myself clearly and in such a way as to be heard by the person I am with. It feels a lot better, both for me and my friends.

Speaking out...

The question is, how do we reconnect with our truth? How do we uncover the layers that mask our true feelings and have the courage to speak about them freely? Like all things, this too is a practice. We begin by stopping for a moment and asking our heart what feels right. We let go of the tendency of allowing our minds to dictate to us, and instead we allow our hearts to guide us, through our feeling nature. Then, we take the risk of expressing what we feel. And we watch what happens. Firstly, do we feel better for having spoken out? Are we more at peace? Secondly, what is the reaction from those around us? In my experience our truth is always the highest truth for those around us who are affected by it, even though this may not appear to be so at the time. Often I have initially been disappointed by someone's decision that was not in line with the way I thought things should happen, only to find later that their decision affected me in a positive way! With this as my experience it is now easier to accept other people's truth, even if my mind may resist it initially.

With others...

Finding ways to speak our truth with sensitivity and clarity helps us to be heard and respected. In integrity we don't attack someone else's position or defend our own, we just say *what is so* for us. Can we have the courage to take a risk in this way and share our truth without worrying about the outcome or what others will think of us? If we are in an uncomfortable situation and feel scared about expressing our truth, one useful tool is to share our vulnerability first and say something like, "I'm scared to say this, but..." When we dare to be vulnerable in this way, the person we are speaking to is going to be a lot more receptive to what we have to say.

Doing and saying things just to please others is living dishonestly and is based in fear. It's a practice of giving ourselves away instead of honoring our own wants and needs. Instead, we must learn to ask for what we want and be prepared to negotiate the response. Our friends cannot read minds. Asking for what we need helps us to take care of ourselves and be responsible for our lives. When we do this, we preclude others from care-taking us, and we eject ourselves firmly from the victim position, resulting in much healthier relationships and more empowerment for all.

Sharing our inner dialogue, the mind chatter that's always present in our heads, is a great tool for keeping us current with our truth. It has the power to liberate our relationships by making us more present in the moment. Obviously some discretion can be used here as to when to speak up. It's not necessary or useful to give a running commentary. A technique that I find works really well here is asking permission to share our thoughts before we do so. This is a nice way to open up a space for honesty and receptivity and reduces the tendency of the other person to get defensive.

Trust is a precious commodity—earn it.

Listen to the words...

Words are important, too. Can every word out of our mouth be one of truth? Any time we lie, we are resisting the world as it is and instead trying to change it to suit our desires. Words have power, so we would do well to use them wisely. If we catch ourselves saying something negative or saying an untruth out loud and wish to negate it, one trick is to just softly say, "Cancel, clear" after the statement and then go on to say what is true. We can become aware of our tendency to exaggerate, too. Are we exaggerating to create more melodrama, to attract attention to ourselves with our "dramatic story?" Instead, we can practice making statements of things just as they are, without embellishment.

Commitments...

From our own experience, we all know who amongst our friends can be relied upon to make arrangements with us and not let us down. We also know who is likely to call at the last moment and cancel on us or be terribly late or get the dates mixed up. Which category do we wish to fall into? Do we want to be a person of honor who can be counted on, or a "flake" with no clear direction? We can choose to be our own knight in shining armor. Our trusty steed is the strength of our word and our lance is the solidarity of our commitment.

We can set an example to others, modeling how it is to be a person of impeccability. Indeed, the person of honor sticks to their commitments even if others do not. Honoring commitments earns us not only the respect of others but also of ourselves, and keeping our word to ourselves is a powerful way to build self-esteem. For example, we decide to start an exercise program. We make a commitment to ourselves to go to the gym three times a week for one month. It feels empowering to have a discipline in this way. After the month is over we can renegotiate our commitment with ourselves, depending on how we feel then.

I make very few decisions in the moment. When I am asked to make an agreement with someone I very often ask for time to think about the agreement and consider it thoroughly before coming to a decision. That way I don't feel pressured, I can feel comfortable about the agreement, and it's easier for me to honor the commitment I make. Or, I set an intention instead. An intention is looser than a commitment. For me it means I will probably do something, but I am not yet 100% sure. Making intentions in unclear situations helps to keep me in my integrity while holding my options open.

The bitter truth is better than a sweet lie.
—Ancient proverb

Being honest...

Honoring our truth also encompasses our sense of right and wrong. We all know instinctively that it is wrong to steal, cheat, and lie, but sometimes the line gets blurred. For example, how many of us that have worked for large companies have made long distance phone calls to friends without direct permission from the boss? Or "borrowed" a stamp? Or used the office copy machine for personal copies? How often do we justify acts like these in our minds as being somehow "OK," even though we have no express permission to do these things? Being fully in integrity means cleaning up our act in all ways, both big and small, so that we do nothing that results in our feeling guilty or "wrong." The pay-off is that we can now get to feel good about who we are, with a clear conscience and peaceful mind.

Here is an example of how this might work. A friend of mine once asked her teacher if it was out of integrity to duplicate audiotapes to give to friends. He replied, "Does it disturb your peace? If it does, don't do it!" She was annoyed with his answer, because now she had to take responsibility for her acts! Before, she had duplicated tapes without a second thought, but now that she is working on her integrity she can no longer ignore the fact that doing this is dishonest and infringes copyright law, depriving the artists of money for their creativity. Now, where possible, she buys new tapes from the record store instead of duplicating onto blanks!

To sum up...

Being in integrity is about acting and speaking honestly. It is also the first step towards feeling "enough." We can have no inner peace if we do not honor ourselves by speaking our truth and being our word. So we feel what our truth is, speak it sensitively, ask for what we want, be our word, and honor our commitments.

> *"...as children we innately felt the rightness and wrongness of whatever was occurring; and only as our perceptions became distorted as to what was right or wrong, based on our confusing conditioning, did we fall out of touch with...our natural ability to discern for ourselves truth and not-truth. We became crippled in our ability to source ourselves. How sad!"*
>
> —IsanaMada, *A Call to Greatness*

Examples:

Many years ago I went on my first yoga retreat with my kundalini yoga teacher, Siri Gian Singh. I loved the experience so much and wanted to go again, but money was tight so I asked him if he would consider a trade of my skills of teaching T'ai Chi and leading the sing-alongs with my guitar in return for a free passage. He very sweetly looked me in the eye and said, "No!" He explained that he already had enough people trading skills with him and really didn't need me as well.

I went home with my tail between my legs and told my husband what had happened. He said, "Why do you think you need him? You can do all he can and more! Start your own retreats!" So I did! And ten years later they are still going strong! So I can now see that Siri Gian speaking his truth, although it was not what

I wanted to hear at the time, ultimately benefited me greatly. I am forever grateful to him for that!

A friend of mine dates a police officer who loves to go to movies. He likes to go to a show in a large movie complex and then sneak in to see one or two more shows immediately after. The first time he tried to do this with my friend, who has a high sense of integrity, she asked if he was going to go outside the complex and pay again to go in. He looked at her strangely. She said, "If you won't be honest about paying to see each movie, who will?" They went outside and paid again.

Pete, a student of mine, had a relative who desperately wanted to be a part of his life. However, in the past this relative had done some things that had upset Pete and his family to the point where Pete no longer wanted to have any contact with the person. Still, the Christmas cards would come and the phone calls, all asking Pete why he wasn't making time in his life to see the relative. This was upsetting to Pete, who was feeling guilty and not at all at peace with the situation.

I asked Pete if he'd ever clearly explained to the person why he wanted to cut him out of his life. He said he hadn't so I suggested he call him and speak his truth—the reasons why he felt the way he did. Pete did that and reported he now felt much clearer and cleaner about the relationship. It had been a completion for both of them. Ostensibly, nothing had changed, but now Pete was at peace.

I once held a workshop at my house which was due to start at 10:00 a.m. People had driven from far away to be there and at 9:45 a.m. everyone had arrived except for a friend of mine who lives five minutes away from my house. I called him. He said he was just leaving. We waited. And waited. It was 10:15 and he still hadn't shown up. I decided to start the opening circle anyway and then he walked in.

During opening circle everyone had a chance to share something about themselves. One man there said he needed to share his feelings with my late friend. He told him that he really wanted to be present with him during the day, but that in order to feel present he had to get something off his chest. He said he felt dishonored by my friend's late arrival, that he had driven from 100 miles away and had made an effort to be there on time, but then we all had had to wait for him. My friend received the sharing gracefully and the day proceeded on. I watched these two men interact during the day and was impressed at how their honest earlier interaction enabled them to be deeply intimate with each other now that their feelings had been truthfully spoken.

> *In integrity there are no insignificant acts. This means that in the eyes of God there is no difference between stealing a cookie and robbing a bank.*

Exercises:

Immediate action:

For one day, watch what comes out of your mouth.

Watch when you are afraid to speak your truth or behave in a way that honors you. Watch the tendency to say things to please others when this may not be an honest answer. Notice how it feels when you withhold and don't ask for what you want, or say an untruth. Where do you feel it in your body?

Ongoing awareness:

Become a person of impeccable integrity. Be your word.

Ram Dass, the well-known spiritual teacher, was giving a lecture. Amidst the New Age seekers, in the front row was a little old lady, sensible shoes and all, smiling and nodding all through the lecture and looking so serene. At the end, Ram Dass approached her and asked her how she liked his lecture. In a knowing way she complimented him on his fine words and understanding of the truth.

"But how do you know all this?" he asked.

She answered, "I crochet."

THERE IS A MONSTER THAT EATS OUR PEACE…

There is a monster called attachment that eats our peace. Its limbs are preference, desire, judgment, and criticism. In the next few chapters we will explore these four limbs and discover ways of freeing ourselves from their all-encompassing grasp.

Attachments are expressions of the ego. They can be either our masters or our servants. We can look at each of these limbs individually as a path towards reducing the influence of the ego in our lives.

Preferences and desires are about what we want. They both imply an attachment to a desired outcome.

Preferences are attachments of the mind, pertaining to external circumstances. We want something to be different than the way it is.

Desires are attachments born within us that have the power to consume us. Many addictions are of this nature. It's about "having to have something."

Judgments involve opinions about *what is so* and attachment to the way we think it should be.

Criticism is an expression of judgment about others that builds the criticizer's ego at the expense of the other person.

The great modern-day sage, Papaji, was asked, "What is the biggest obstacle to enlightenment?" "Attachment," he replied, without hesitation!

5
What's the preference?

Helps free us from disappointments

Life used to be simple. When we lived in primitive cultures, we ate only a few basic foods, we all lived in simple shelters, and we wore the same fashions. Having lots of preferences wasn't an issue, as the choices were simply not there in the first place.

In our contemporary, materialistic world we are inundated with choice. We can choose our jobs, our food, our clothing, even our mates, which makes it more likely for us to have preferences about our possible choices and to compare what we don't have to what others have.

Preferences are about having things "our way." The more preferences we have, and the more we are attached to them, the greater our potential for unhappiness. Often our expectations will not be met, and we'll be faced with the alternatives to deal with. In this way preferences are the source of our dissatisfaction. We don't get what we want, and everything else is "less than." The extreme example of this is the perfectionist who cannot be happy until all circumstances in life are the way he wants them. As this can never happen, that person will always be dealing with unhappiness and dissatisfaction, unable to see the sacredness of life the way it is.

Expectations...

Preferences involve expectations of how we want things to be in the future and resistance to how well our expectations match up with reality. That is, resistance to *"what's so."* The more detailed the pictures in our head of how we expect things to be, and the more attached we are to these pictures, the more we set ourselves up for disappointment and sorrow. It can feel uncomfortable to be around people with rigid expectations. Even if not voiced, we sense their underlying feelings of displeasure when things do not go their way. People like this are hard to please and are often miserable, locked into the prison of their own rigidity.

Instead of having expectations, we can set intentions for the way we would like things to be, but hold on to those intentions lightly, keeping an open mind and just appreciating what shows up. This changes our whole experience of life, as we get to be delighted with what is, instead of disappointed with what we think "should have been."

Resistance...

Western culture trains us to have preferences. We are encouraged to want a picture-perfect world, with dream vacations, loving partners, happy families, and beautiful homes. When our lives don't match the images in our imaginations, we complain, exhibiting what we might call "Spoiled Brat Syndrome." Little kids have lots of preferences. They don't yet have the maturity of acceptance. Kids throw temper tantrums. Sometimes adults do, too, because like the child, they want their own way and resist accepting reality as different than their wants and desires. These types of people complain, are picky and opinionated, and are generally not fun to be around. We all have the capacity to be that way, but part of maturity is choosing to not react like a child when preferences aren't met.

On a more subtle level, we can notice when we make statements such as "I hate it when," "I think it should be...," and "I wish it were..." as evidence of having preference. Activating our witness consciousness here and watching our tendencies to make these statements is a start in letting go of our resistance to life as it is.

What you resist persists.

Stuck in a rut...

Preferences are the ego's way of wanting to control the world. For example, we recall how great a certain thing was and want it to be that way again. I always look forward to going to a hot springs spa where I like to have a massage from a certain therapist. Before, if he was not available when I would go there, I had to deal with my feelings of disappointment instead of looking to see if another experience with someone else was waiting to happen. Now I have no preference around who is there to give me a massage. I trust that the therapist who shows up is the perfect one for me at the time.

Preferences can also keep us stuck in ruts, repeating the same old patterns in our lives, eating the same food, and going to the same vacation spots, instead of being open to explore more possibilities. When I worked for a publishing company in London, I used to travel abroad a lot with my boss. He would only order steak from the menu, no matter where we were or how delicious the local food! He never liked to try "foreign food," and definitely exhibited a preference to English-style cuisine! In this way his preferences allowed him to feel safe in his world but limited his experience of more exciting taste treats!

No room for preference...

Traveling in poor countries where our taken-for-granted luxuries of daily living just don't exist helped me to let go of a lot of my preferences. There simply was no choice; I just had to deal with what was available at the time. I remember trying to wash my hair from a bucket of cold water in the mountains of Nepal, and I was grateful there was water for washing at all; eating plain lentils and rice in the deserts of Rajasthan in India, and I was grateful that there was food to eat at all.

Watching how the richer, more privileged tourists dealt with these austerities was a source of amusement for us shoestring travelers. It was so clear how their attitude of preference would cause them distress and make them miserable in a situation where we were having a ball and enjoying the adventure of our new experiences.

I am reminded here, too, of the movie "The Hurricane." When Hurricane Carter was sent to prison, he decided to have no more room in his life for preferences that could cause him additional pain. So he voluntarily withdrew from prison exercise, social events, and other prison privileges, reasoning that if he rejected them from the beginning they could not be taken away and would therefore have no power over him.

Preference v. choice...

We rarely let go of all preferences completely. Instead, we can move towards bringing our preferences as much into the present time as possible and loosening the grip of our rigid attachment to them. When we do that, they transform into a choice. A choice takes place in the moment. For example, we go to a restaurant and we need to make a choice about what to eat, now. The salmon sounds good so we order that. Or we have a shopping list for vegetables but notice once we get to the store that we are drawn to purchase the zucchini that looks particularly fresh rather than the sad looking broccoli that was on our list.

Staying empowered...

There is a fine line between letting go of our preferences and giving up our power. Honoring the body's physical needs for food, sleep and rest is not about having a preference. It is about looking after ourselves. Similarly, in our relationships, when faced with a choice, it is a place of empowerment to follow our heart's wisdom rather than continually going along with what other people want. Perhaps I like to live life spontaneously, but my partner likes to plan everything to the smallest detail. I like the house neat and tidy, but my partner feels more comfortable with mess and chaos abounding. What to do? Stating our preferences and negotiating would be appropriate here. We are not being asked to become subservient in order to please others. Listening to our inner voice about what is best for us and making choices based on those gut feelings is an act of self-love that empowers us to stand in our highest truth.

Acceptance...

When we are attached to our preferences we resist the flow of life. Imagine floating down the river and instead of flowing with the current (life), we are trying to grab on to the roots hanging from the riverbank, struggling to hold on. The opposite of preference is acceptance of the way things are and being OK with that, saying "yes" to all of our experiences as they occur, feeling all of them as much as possible, with full awareness. When we are more accepting, we are less angry, less upset. We are happier. The result is a softer us, less hard around the edges.

In ancient India, the people were more connected with their spiritual nature, so in order to perform austerities to demonstrate their love of God, it was necessary to lie on a bed of nails or wear a hair coat. Nowadays, just going to the mall with limited cash can be an austerity!

Examples:

When I take yoga classes I often notice my preference around being able to perform all the asanas that are being taught. After all, I am a yoga teacher. I should be able to do them all! However, I still cannot sit in lotus position! But now, after working with this issue, I am able to let go of my preference and accept and love my body the way it is.

Many people have preference around timing. "I want enlightenment and I want it now!" Instead, can we be grateful for how far we've come along the path?

My friend Alan's wife used to be very overweight. This weight gain had occurred over a number of years, and as the pounds piled on, Alan became more and more discontented with his wife's appearance. In an attempt to manipulate the situation he would offer "rewards" for pounds lost and threaten penalties for pounds gained. All this had no effect on her. After some years, Alan let go of his preference and decided to just love his wife exactly as she was, fat or not. Miraculously, once this energy of preference was diminished, his wife no longer felt pressured to lose weight. And the pounds dropped off quite naturally!

My ex-partner wanted a vegetarian for a girlfriend. He definitely had an expectation around it but when he met me, I was not a vegetarian! We fell in love and he decided to let go of his preference in order to be with me.

One time during an outdoor yoga class, a chain saw started up next door, creating all kinds of noise! Instead of getting upset about the noise, our teacher invited us to hear it as an "om machine." That helped me to let go of my preference about having quiet for the class.

Many of us have preferences about being sick or injured. We would rather have energy and be active. But if we can let go of that preference and accept our times of illness gracefully we will often find value for ourselves in having quiet time to rest and be still, an invitation to slow down and go within.

Exercises:

Immediate action:

Start to notice your preferences today. Pay attention to when your preferences do not get met and how that feels.

Notice how it is to be around people who complain all the time (that is, they have a lot of preferences) as opposed to those who are easy-going.

Ongoing awareness:

Begin to cultivate an attitude of gracious acceptance instead of preference. Embrace the flow of life!

To take this to a deeper level, become aware of preference as an outpouring of the individual ego's will, in contrast to the Divine Will, as manifested by what shows up.

> *"Drop character. Be fluid, more flowing, live moment to moment. It does not mean irresponsibility; it means greater responsibility because it means greater awareness....when you don't have any hard structure around you, you have to be alert each moment....each moment you have to respond to the new situation....how can you respond in a new way? ...Be characterless, be without character. Characterlessness is freedom."* —Osho

6

What's the desire?

Aligns us with our true purpose

In India there is a story about a holy man who desired enlightenment for six years with no success. Then one day, weak from fasting, he went to a river to bathe. As the water rushed over his weakened body, he felt moved to surrender and relinquish his search for God. He returned to sit under his bodhi tree and in this place of desirelessness he was finally graced with enlightenment.

So how do we achieve this desireless state? Isn't it a contradiction in terms to desire desirelessness? This arena of inquiry is a minefield of contradictions, confusion and controversy. The Buddhist approach has been to observe worldly desires as they arise, and continue to watch them until they pass. The yogic and Christian approach has been to suppress desires. The tantric approach is to embrace desires, satisfying them fully. In all these approaches the futility of worldly desires is eventually realized and all desires finally fall away. What remains is a pure state of desirelessness, where the person can be offered up as a servant to God with no other agenda, except to carry out the Divine Will.

Ego-desire vs. godly desire...

Desire is not bad. We need it to push us into gaining precious experiences of life. We are all born with desire. Desire comes from the inside out. It is an inner urge that tells us we have to have something. We feel it in our body. It propels us to act to fulfill the desire. Without desire the world would come to a standstill. We would be lethargic and uninventive. Very dull! What gets us into trouble is our relationship to our desires and how attached we are to having them fulfilled.

Ego-driven desire involves attachment to the outcome of our activities. It comes from our own free will, from our minds, which tell us that we have to have all kinds of things, pleasures, and sensations to make us happy. Most of us listen to these desires and follow the path of indulgence for a while, allowing our desires to run our world. We have goals to achieve, experiences to enjoy and dreams we want to realize, until we understand that these ego-driven desires give us only temporary happiness and satisfaction. That's when we are ripe for a quantum change in our life.

Pure desire comes from God and helps us to carry out the function of creation. We can call this inspiration, our attraction to our destiny. We are moved from within to act in certain ways, drawn to certain people and activities, and in so doing feel a sense of fulfillment and satisfaction, as the force of the desire aligns us with our life-path. When we can discern the source of our desire and have the experience that doing God's Will gives us more satisfaction than following our own, then our lives can change dramatically as we listen to the wisdom from within guiding our every move.

Bright and shiny baubles...

Desire is a place I know well. As a hedonistic thrill seeker I have flung myself out of moving airplanes, bungee-jumped off cliffs, rafted wild waters, and hitchhiked around the world, mostly solo. At school I was taught to be competitive, to achieve goals as the mark of success. So I set about getting the best degree, obtaining the most exciting job, and acquiring the trappings of success. I did all of these things, played them out to their fullest, and enjoyed the many and varied experiences that I had along the way. My worldly desires have been fully realized, so I have no regrets. Indeed, I celebrated every step of the beautiful journey of my life. But as I grew older I came to realize that these self-pleasuring external activities no longer fulfilled me. So what if I lived in a nice house? So what if I have traveled around the world a number of times? Those desires, once played out, gave me no lasting joy. However, I allowed myself to indulge them fully, until I had enough. Then they fell away of their own accord.

I began to realize that this urge for thrills and goals came from a place of not feeling fulfilled inside. Desiring more and more external experiences distracted me from the emptiness of the present. I wanted to fill that empty space with something that would get me excited enough to alter my feeling state. It took much practice of yoga and meditation for that need to finally be resolved. Now I feel full and complete just as I am, by being as present and conscious as possible in every moment. I accept myself fully and have nothing more to prove. Desires still come and go. Now I observe and evaluate them before pushing myself to realize them.

These days I am driven by a desire to serve, to share experiences with others and to build community and nurture friendships. The desire to write this book has been a part of that. My ego-self could think of many more fun things to do than sit in front of the computer all day and write! But I have to do it—the inner desire to share the tools in this book is so strong that there is no other choice of action.

One clue as to whether desire comes from God or ego-self is the sense of satisfaction and contentment obtained from playing out the desire. When I write I feel completely at peace and nurtured by the process. It feels like the right action for the day, as though purpose is being fulfilled. It makes me feel truly alive. The sun may be shining but I would rather sit inside and write this than hike in the mountains or play in the river. And that sense of satisfaction lasts beyond the moment, helping me to feel at peace in my life and with the direction my life is taking.

Goals and plans...

Most of us have goals and dreams that give us direction. While it is fine to make plans to fulfill our dreams, over-attachment to goals takes our focus away from being present in the moment and instead holds our happiness ransom to a mythical future time. If we are fixated on these dreams coming into fulfillment in order to be happy, we set ourselves up for failure and disappointment. We are imposing conditions on our happiness, constantly waiting for something "better" to show up. In the meantime we are missing the main act, our life in the present moment.

Our culture in the western world encourages our material desires. We see advertising pictures of happy families with their large houses and fancy cars. We are taught to believe that if only we had those things that we, too, would be happy and fulfilled like the people in the picture. While there is nothing wrong with having nice things to enjoy and to make our lives easier, the trap here is that we tend to get fixated on those dreams, to the exclusion of all else. Instead of being grateful for what we have now, there is a sense of discontent. But as many millionaires will tell us, when the thrill of the material acquisitions has worn off, they are generally still not satisfied. So the striving continues and may continue until death unless the person comes to an understanding as to what is really behind the source of the discontent.

When we are fully conscious in the present moment, nothing is lacking. We are already rich in our experience, feeling our life fully. We feel whole, full, and complete, no matter what our external circumstance. Striving falls away and instead guidance shows up. As we become more conscious our desires fall into alignment with God's Will for us, our divine purpose, which in turn gives us deep satisfaction and fulfillment in our lives. The endless cycle of ego-driven desire begins to fade, and instead our desires become our servant rather than our master.

> *"Desire is the root of all suffering."*
> —The Buddha

Desire as our servant...

Our desires can serve us in many different ways. For example, when we have divine inspiration, spirit propels us into action. A thought of a goal or dream comes in. We make a plan around the thought to bring it into manifestation. We pay attention to see if universal energy supports our plan. If it does, the plan will manifest with complete integrity, even though we will be required to go through the motions around this manifestation. If not, we let it go without attachment. In this way, divine inspiration guides us instinctively into the unknown future without fear of failure. We allow ourselves to follow impulses of intuition rather than listening to the controlling ego-mind.

The desire for survival and good health supports us in taking care of our physical needs, like getting plenty of rest, eating well to support the body functions, and drinking plenty of water. We all desire companionship and are thus encouraged to understand relationships! My desire for travel eventually led me to find my true spiritual home in Northern California. These are just a few examples of how desires guide us in our lives, helping us to bring forth the highest level of expression of ourselves as humans.

The seven deadly sins...

Let's take a look at the underlying desires of our base nature, the human part of us that feels lust, greed, laziness, avarice... the seven deadly sins, and the day-to-day desires with which we are all familiar, the desire for ice cream, fine wine, sexual fulfillment, companionship. What do we do with these desires as they arise?

First we must acknowledge them, accept them, and honor them. Then we can investigate them. Is this really what we want right now? Where is this desire sourced? What is behind it? How does it feel to indulge in the desire? Notice that in this investigation there is no judgment present, just curiosity. If we resist the desire and push it away, we are not accepting a part of our humanness. How can we be whole if we do not accept a part of ourselves? This investigation is how we shine the light of our awareness on our behavior. Then if we choose to indulge our desires, we feel fully how it is for us. Very often, if we do this, our desires will change and a new awareness and understanding will arise.

Addictions...

The extreme expression of base nature desire is addiction, such as to cigarettes or alcohol, where the inner urges consume us and run our lives. Addictions are a great avoidance mechanism. When we indulge our addictions, unconsciously it's a demonstration that we are unwilling to get our lessons. However, if we will only stop and take a look at the underlying cause of the addiction and see what triggers it, we have the opportunity to expand our awareness and understand ourselves more deeply. We can shine the light of awareness upon our addictions without judgment, to examine their purpose. If it is not immediately clear, we can ask God to reveal it. Then, once we have learned all there is from the addiction, we are ready to release it.

Addictions may serve us for a time until we develop new skills to handle the causes of the addiction. For example, consider the alcoholic who uses alcohol to relieve stress. It may be better for that person to calm down by drinking than to have a heart attack by getting over-anxious! But better still to learn some stress-reducing techniques that would alleviate the need for drinking alcohol altogether.

Any addiction pushed away before its time will only return. However, once the desire has been fully played out and understood, it will drop away on its own accord without being pushed away. My girlfriend used to smoke two packs of cigarettes a day. However, she also practiced yoga with me and came on my yoga vacation to the Yucatan one year. After dinner it was her habit to get up and leave the table to go have a cigarette. One evening as she left to do this she had a moment of epiphany. She felt the pain of leaving the happy gathering just to indulge her habit. This prompted her to spend some quiet time during the rest of the vacation investigating her addiction. She discovered that she smoked out of a sense of insecurity. When she was eventually able to release this feeling and replace it with feelings of fullness and love, the nicotine cravings left. She stopped smoking immediately after the trip was over, effortlessly and easily, and has not missed it at all!

If we have an addictive personality we can use it to thrive by substituting our unhealthy addictions for healthy ones! Instead of being addicted to doughnuts and television we could develop a passion for a raw foods diet, a yoga practice, or the search for Self-realization.

Habitual patterns...

Habits and desires feed each other by fostering unconscious behavior. Noticing our habit patterns and moving away from them is a great way to release the grip of the desire. For example, I come home every afternoon and put the kettle on and eat chocolate with my tea. I notice that if I don't put the kettle on, my desire for the chocolate falls away. So if we start to alter our habitual everyday activities or environments, we stand a far greater chance of letting go of unwanted desires. The great Indian guru Yogananda used to say that environment is ten times stronger than willpower! That is, the company we keep is a great influence on our behavior. So it's a good idea to hang out with people whose lifestyles you wish to emulate rather than be with people who have habits that we are trying to break away from.

The subtle level....

When we are experiencing the fullness of the moment, desire drops away completely. We feel full with ourselves, and there is nothing lacking. Only gratitude shows up.

> *"Lord, put me where it is you want me to be, with whom it is you want me to be, doing what it is you want me to be doing. Let thy will be mine..."*
> —Yogi's prayer

Examples:

I used to live in a big house, the "mansion" we called it! It had an enormous empty yard just perfect for a pool, and before I moved in I was already dreaming about the swimming that I would enjoy there! My partner, who owned the house, wanted to design a fantastic ornate garden around the pool with streams, waterfalls, the works! It became a very complicated project, and the result was that the project just never got done. I didn't get the pool that I wanted. I got quite upset about this. The expectation that I was attached to remained unfulfilled. My ego-driven desires remained thwarted. Circumstances changed. My partner and

I split up and I realized I would have to move out of the house. I suddenly shifted my attitude and was no longer concerned about not having a pool but instead appreciated more fully every day I got to spend in that beautiful place.

I make long-term plans to host yoga retreats. I try to have no attachment to their success and instead offer the work up as a service. If a group of people sign up for the retreat, it is clear that I am being asked to do it. If not, I cancel the event without taking it personally.

I recently bought a house. I had desired a three-bedroom house with pool (of course!) in my favorite part of Sacramento. With the money I had to spend, this looked like an impossible dream. Still, I was clear on my vision and prayed for guidance during the house-buying process. Then a miracle occurred. My realtor found a house that met all my criteria at an unbelievable price! I rushed over to see it and cried when I saw it—it was so perfect! The house had multiple offers on it but the seller's realtor told my realtor she had a strange feeling that I was meant to have the house! My offer ended up being the one that was accepted. I was so thrilled and could totally see the hand of the Divine in the process of finding my perfect residence! In this case, my desire was supported by the universe, and as such was in line with God's Will for me.

> *"Attachments are the ego's riveting desires which have become obsessive attempts to control relationships and circumstances."*
> —IsanaMada, *A Call to Greatness*

Exercises:

Immediate action:

Begin an investigation of your addictions and habits. Notice if these habits support you or not. See what triggers them, how you feel before, during, and after.

Ongoing awareness:

Look at your long-term goals and plans. Were these divine inspirations or do they come from a place of ego and attachment? Learn to hold on to your long-term goals lightly.

"Now you don't have any goals, now you don't have any desires to fulfill, you don't have any future. You are just here now. When the energy has become a pool, not going anywhere, not flowing anywhere; no goal to be attained, nothing to be sought, you are just here, tremendously here, totally here; this now is all the time that is left for you, and this here is all the space. Then suddenly this gathering of energy, which is not moving anywhere, not distracted by body or mind, becomes a great rush in you. And...the one-thousand-petal-lotus opens." —Osho

7

What's the judgment?

Frees us from limiting belief systems

For many of us our inner judges have been entrenched in our psyche and in charge of our lives for many years! Living in a society that constantly judges everything and everyone reinforces this "normal" behavior. It is a hard habit to break, but break it we must, in order to free ourselves from the judge's tight grasp on our belief systems.

Judgment is...

Judgment has one or more of the following four characteristics:

- It has an opinion about *what is so.* For example, "Poor Mary, she hurt her back in a car accident yesterday. How awful."
- It involves either a preference about something or an attachment to an outcome. For example, I was very sad when I lost my house to foreclosure years ago and judged it as a "bad" thing. I was very attached to staying in the house. How could I have known then that it was exactly what I needed in order to break free from an unfulfilling life?
- It is a morality of the mind regarding the polar opposites of what is good and bad, right and wrong. We live in a world of duality, and these morality judgments help to anchor us there. For example, "Jane is a good mother." "It is wrong to fight."
- It's a stimulus-reaction from our past, a preconditioned idea. For example, coming as I do from England, I have a tendency to look out on a rainy day and think how miserable it is, as I hook into all those occasions in my past when "rain stopped play."

The price we pay...

When we judge, certain things can happen. Judgment carries an emotional charge that creates a contraction in the physical body, a tension in the muscles that locks us down. This doesn't feel good! If we can become aware of this contraction at the time, we have the opportunity to let go of the judgment and release it. Otherwise, this contraction will stay in our body in the form of tight muscles, that we sometimes call "armoring."

When we judge based on a reaction from our past, our choice is removed, as we don't see any other ways to respond. We tend to think that our assumptions are true, which limits our reality of what's possible. Instead, we remain fixed and rigid in our position, locked in to being "right" at the expense of making new choices. For example, when I first learned yoga I was taught a certain way to do shoulder stand. Later in my yoga career I came across teachers who did it differently than me and in my mind I judged them as "wrong," because I assumed the way I had been taught was the "right and only" way. Of course, this attitude limited my ability to explore new techniques.

Judging can isolate us from others and block us from friendships. For example, when we judge someone else as inferior in any way, it alienates us from that person and the friendship and love that are available. Most people have a tendency to judge by appearances. We think that a person is fat and therefore lazy, or ugly and therefore unattractive. Think how often we initially judge people in a negative way, only later to wind up good friends with that person once we get to know them better!

When we judge others we create an energy field that attracts judgment to ourselves. This can be in the form of judgment from others or the tendency to self-judge. We are often far harder on ourselves than we would be towards friends and acquaintances. When the voice of our internal critic is active it is very difficult for us to truly love and accept ourselves as we are.

Judgment denies God...

Too often we have a tendency to accept God into our lives

and pray to our Creator but not accept the Creation. The Creator and the Creation are one. Clinging to one aspect of our world and judging it as "good" and rejecting what we don't like as "bad" stems from our ego-self and essentially says "no" to God. This does not mean that we should not help people in need, but that we keep observing *what's so* without a judgment on whether what is happening is good or bad. Our opinion is not going to change anything anyway. Only our actions will do that.

Judgment as opportunity...

Judging others is a sign that there's something about ourselves we do not feel good about, so it's an indication that we need to take a look at ourselves and see why we have a need to think this way. For example, we see someone getting angry with their child and hitting them in the shopping mall. We jump to judgment as to how awful it is that this mother could hit her child. If this judgment really creates a charge inside of us, it is an indication that there is a part of us that needs healing, a part of us deep inside that we have not embraced and accepted. In this case, it may be our capacity to show anger. Judgments where our buttons are really getting pushed can point to our undiscovered shadow side and can be an exciting journey of detective work for those of us prepared to delve deeply into our psyche!

Whose judgment is it?...

Very often we hold on to the opinions of what we have heard other people say. We carry the judgments of our parents and teachers with us as we grow up, and jump into them automatically without examining if they are really ours.

Prejudices are often of this nature. Maybe our father taught us to be suspicious of people from foreign countries or with different color skins. With no grounds for this belief we paint all people in that category with the same brush. Our work as mature adults is to look at these old belief systems and start to dissolve them, as we continue to open our hearts to love and acceptance of all that is.

Compliments...

But what about compliments and praise, you might ask? Well, in a way they too are judgments. We live in a world of duality and polarity, which is by definition a world of judgment. The duality becomes part of our social conversation. "My, what a nice dress." "That's a great new car you have!" They are not wrong, but there is a way to change the energy of our remarks. We can express the compliments as a feeling that we have, which then becomes our truth. For example, "It feels really exciting for me when your car accelerates so quickly." Or, "I really like the colors in your dress."

A friend of mine recently told me a story about how one day her five-year-old child was doing art with a playmate who received praise from his mother for a drawing he had done. Her child started to cry. When she asked him what was wrong he said, "Tom's mom said his drawing was good and she didn't tell me that, so it must mean that mine is bad!" Sometimes it takes the mind of a child to point out the obvious—that when we compliment in this way we infer that everything else is not as good. Also, when we praise a child for doing something, they make the connection between praise and activity; that is, that they need to do something to earn our love. Instead we might look to observe their emotional state and comment on that. For example, we might say, "Look how happy you are when you paint!"

Judgment vs. observation...

Observation is about *what is so.* Unlike judgment it carries no emotional charge. It is dispassionate, neutral. When we turn judgment of the world around us into observation there is no contraction in the body, no tension. There is just a noticing of the way things are without opinion, story, or agenda. Like a camera taking a snapshot of a slice of existence, we notice *what's so* and leave it at that. This is empowering and liberating. We can now move towards a place of faith that everything is fine just the way it is, which deepens our practice of acceptance and non-resistance.

Judgment vs. discernment and experience...

There is a difference between being judgmental and being discerning. Discernment is looking to see *what's so* and making decisions and choices based on the facts. We could also call this an assessment or value judgment. For example, we meet someone initially and judge them on face value of what we see before us and our limited experience of them. Then, after a few years of knowing the person, if someone were to ask us if that person were suitable for a job taking care of elderly people, we may assess their personality and skill-set as we have experienced them and make an assessment based on that.

A judge has to listen carefully to the facts of the case and make a decision accordingly. One judge I know puts it this way. "The people who come before my bench have earned the right to be there. They are aware of the possible consequences. Who am I to come between them and their path? My job is to hold the space safe and sacred for those involved so the truth can be revealed. In that place my duty is to remain clear, neutral, and objective."

Judgments are opinions that reside in our heads. They are not the same as experiences that we feel in our bodies and hearts. When we feel something, it is our truth and is not a judgment. Instead it is our experience. For example, we all know some people who talk incessantly, leaving no gaps for real conversation. It is my experience that when I am around a person like that I feel that they are talking at me, not to me, and I am often left feeling drained and tired. There is a difference between labeling a person as a "chatterbox" and remarking that in their presence we feel tired and disempowered.

Letting go of judgments...

Once again we enlist the help of our witness consciousness to notice when a judgment pops into our heads and what happens in our bodies as a result. The more conscious we become of this, the quicker we catch our judgments arising and the easier it is to just let them go. With time, the more we heal ourselves from our past conditioning, the more our judgments start to shift naturally into neutral observations.

Ultimately…

Eventually judgment drops away altogether and we only see *what is so,* as the world is presented to us moment by moment. We stop evaluating. The opposites of duality have merged to form harmony and unity.

All paths are valid.

Examples:

I used to have a commute to work that involved driving down what I considered to be the ugliest, busiest freeway I had ever encountered, Highway 880 in Oakland. As soon as I would turn onto it I would often get stuck in slow-moving traffic and have plenty of time to gaze upon the dilapidated warehouses and ugly shopping centers that lined the freeway. I could feel my body tighten in preparation for what seemed like the interminable crawl towards my destination. After a while I became aware of my reaction and didn't like the energy of judgment that I was experiencing. I asked a wise friend of mine about a way to shift it for myself. He said, "There's nothing that's not God—even the graffiti-laden walls of the old buildings you see. It's a part of the wondrous creation, in all its ugliness!" Bearing that in mind, the next time I drove the 880 freeway I was able to look around at the scene in front of me with compassion for the way it was. I relaxed, and my slow crawl seemed to go a little faster!

One night I was cooking an elaborate dinner for my partner. He was due to arrive at 7 p.m. By 8 he still had not called or arrived. I was upset and angry, and definitely inclined to judge. At 8:15 when I heard his car pull up, I decided that by judging his behavior and being mad with him I would spoil our evening and upset myself even more. Instead I chose to turn it into an observation of, "He's over an hour late, that's what's so." When he arrived, I hugged him and then told him I'd been feeling angry and concerned as to his whereabouts and next time would he please call me if he was running so late. I then heard his explanation and let it go at that. There was nothing more to be said or done. We went on to enjoy a beautiful evening.

My friend Eric often talks about his struggle with "spiritual arrogance." As a yogi who has come a long way down the path of conscious awareness, he is tempted to judge people not living in the same way. For example, he feels a big emotional charge of judgment when driving down a certain street packed with fast-food restaurants, watching all the people lining up to "pollute" their bodies with shakes, fries, and burgers. Activating his witness and observing his reaction, he did not like what was happening inside himself. Now his practice is to bless these fast-food establishments for the function that they serve, and work on letting go of his judgments around how bad he thinks the food can be for people.

Exercises:

Specific exercise:

When you notice yourself having a judgment today, first, check inside your body and see where you feel yourself tighten. Next, ask where this judgment came from. "Is it mine?" Then see if this judgment is inviting you to look at an unaccepted part of yourself that you have hitherto been unwilling to embrace. Finally, look again at the judgment and see what has changed.

Ongoing awareness:

When you observe yourself thinking about someone in a judgmental way, immediately counteract it with a blessing. Just think "Bless them!" and send the person that positive thought instead.

Six-year-old Jeremy was upset with his playmate for cheating at a game. He felt angry and ran inside his house, confused and hurt. His grandfather was sitting at the kitchen table, drinking tea.

"What's the matter Jeremy?" asked grandfather.

"Oh Grandpa, I'm angry with my friend and I don't like this feeling. How do I make it go away?"

"Let me tell you about my pet dragons," said Grandpa. "Inside of me I have two dragons. One is

accepting, kind, and compassionate. The other is full of anger, hostility, and judgment. Sometimes they fight each other for my attention."

"Which one wins?" asked Jeremy.

"The one I feed," replied Grandpa.

8

What's the criticism?

Helps us relate to others

Being criticized hurts. When we are criticized we feel we have done something wrong. We feel diminished and unaccepted, which makes us want to be defensive or resentful. It takes away our feeling of safety with the criticizer. We feel attacked, not sure of when the next missile will be launched. This often results in a breakdown of communication and trust, because the person being criticized soon stops sharing information with the criticizer. In this way, criticism creates separation between people, rather than helping us to feel unified and loving.

When I was criticized, my first reaction was to shut down emotionally and retreat within, where I could nurse my wounds in silence. Now I don't take criticism quite so personally, and I try to keep the communication open by letting the criticizer know at the time that what they have said has hurt my feelings. However, it still takes a huge surge of awareness for me to do this rather than to go unconscious and shut down or be defensive when that moment of criticism occurs. This is the gift that everyday life offers us. Each time we are criticized, we get yet another opportunity to raise our consciousness and respond differently, instead of reacting from our usual place of defensiveness.

The cost of criticism...

Criticism is an expression of judgment about others, an assertion of moral superiority. It is an attack that builds the ego at the expense of the other person. That is, we put others down so that we can feel better. However, when we criticize others we actually hurt ourselves on a very deep level. This includes the practice of gossiping and backbiting. In the quantum world of our collective consciousness we are all connected, and any thought sent out across the ether to another has an impact, both for them and for us.

My experience is that when I am being critical it is as though a dark cloud descends upon me. I am aware that it is not feeling good for me to be indulging in the criticism, but sometimes I do not have the willpower to stop. The more I can feel the truth of "when we hurt others we hurt ourselves too," the easier it is for me to catch myself wanting to criticize. Then I can change my behavior.

Recently I have been noticing that when I am critical of someone else I will often exhibit the same behavior shortly afterwards! For example, I was at the airport, and a little kid not paying attention walked right into me. I felt irritated. "Why can't he look where he's going?" I thought. Guess what? Five minutes later I did exactly the same thing myself! I was looking up at the announcement boards and walked into a post! What a lesson in humility! I got to see clearly how the traits we criticize in others are contained in us, too.

I went to a lecture recently where the speaker was talking about how criticism weighs us down, that the critical mind creates an energy of heaviness that is literally "a downer." The same speaker said, "Lovers wear smiles, critics wear frowns." God meant for us to be lovers in the world so we can see each other in our highest light and hold a vision of each other there, like a prayer. I am reminded of stories of how kids growing up in critical households who are told that they will never amount to anything often turn to a life of crime and struggle, as though to validate that message. But when these same kids are exposed to mentors who hold a vision for them of a higher possibility, these kids often rise to the occasion and turn their lives around.

There is a woman in our community whose name is Mary, who works with troubled teenagers. One girl came into her care who was an incorrigible prostitute, even proud of it! Mary kept saying to her that she was a lady, and ladies behave differently than that. The girl never forgot this and took Mary's message into her heart. This positive message helped her to change her ways, and many years later, Mary received a letter from this girl who said she was now married with children and finally felt like a "lady!"

Straight talk...

We all know people who love to complain about others. They will talk for hours about how terrible their husband/boss/girlfriend is, getting us to sympathize and support them in their complaints. Looking for validation and approval for their thoughts and feelings, they suck others into their own melodrama of life. Like the proverbial bad apple, one person's negative energy can infect the rest of a group if not counteracted, and a downward spiral of dark moods will prevail.

Rather than criticizing and complaining to others about someone, it is always better to go to the source, to the person involved, and clear the air with them directly. This saves everyone's energy and honors all concerned. It stops us spinning our wheels and making assumptions about what someone else is thinking or feeling and certainly spares the ears and energy of our friends. We might ask here what kind of interaction we wish to have with our friends and confidants. Do we wish to spend time with them complaining about others in our lives or do we prefer to spend our time with them in more fulfilling ways?

When we do take that time to confront someone, we can bring our complaints into the subjective by making "I" statements. "When you do this, I feel that." Then it no longer becomes a complaint or a criticism. It is just our truth. We are no longer making someone else responsible for our feelings, as we would if we said, "You make me feel..."

Strategies for dealing with critics...

So what can we do around people who criticize and complain? First, we do not have to buy into their criticisms. It is not our job to boost their self-esteem by validating their negative thought patterns. Instead, we can choose to make positive statements to counteract their negative ones, so as to guide them by our example. Sometimes when I am leading groups to warmer climates, there are people who complain about the heat or the mosquitoes. I choose to ignore their complaints, as there is nothing I can do about these things, and instead I gently point out the beauty of things like the sunset and the tropical flowers, guiding their awareness towards things that make them happy instead of upset.

The second possibility is to sit the criticizer down and ask them what is really going on for them at a deeper level. Unhappy people criticize and complain! When given the opportunity to delve into the source of their dissatisfaction, people often unearth hidden feelings of frustration, unworthiness, or lack of love in their lives. Often we just want to be heard and have the chance to express ourselves to another person, and this alone can shift our tendency to criticize.

One of my friends has a husband who used to come home from work and be constantly critical of her. He would launch into a barrage of demands and complaints over silly little stuff, like why the towel was not folded properly in the bathroom. My friend would defend herself vigorously but began to feel hurt, unloved, and unappreciated. She put up with this behavior for a while until one day she was so upset she had just had enough. So she asked him what was really happening with him that he was in such a bad mood. Her husband stopped in his tracks and thought for a minute, then began to tell her that he was going through a very frustrating time at work and felt a lot of anger that he could not express in the workplace. In that moment he realized he was taking the anger out on her in the form of criticism. This awareness helped both of them break their patterns—for him, the pattern of dishing out anger inappropriately, and for her, the pattern of taking the criticism with defensiveness.

There is another option, too. If the first two strategies do not work, then run the other way as quickly as possible! There is no reason why we should stick around negative people who are not willing to change!

What's the agenda?...

Some people like to make the excuse that they are giving "constructive criticism." However the value of this really depends on the intention and agenda of the giver. If they are coming from a place of judgment and trying to make us wrong in some way, then it falls under the same category of just plain "criticism." If there is an emotional charge around what they say, then this may be coloring their perceptions. However, if the person is coming from a place of love, humility and objectivity, with no attachment to outcome, then the criticism can well be constructive and useful. Our challenge here is to examine the prejudices of the giver enough to be able to discern what is truly useful for us. We must learn to trust ourselves to pull out the nuggets of truth without taking the criticism personally, taking responsibility for what is ours, and letting go of the rest.

Criticism vs. feedback...

Criticism is different than feedback or input. Feedback is a process that leads to growth, gives people tools, and builds trust, and is not done for personal gain. Feedback is often requested; that is, there is an agreement between the people concerned that input will be given. Rather than diminish, this empowers the student. The person giving the feedback ideally has no attachment to outcome and no agenda around what is being shared. For example, I asked a friend of mine to review this book before I sent it to the publisher. I gave her full permission to speak freely from her heart. She did, and I learned a lot from her opinions, even though they were not exactly what I wanted to hear!

Asking before sharing feedback is a very powerful tool that honors everyone. I find that when a friend asks to share something with me, I am far more inclined to listen carefully and with an open mind than if I just get blasted with a criticism. Also, if my friend asks to share something and I am feeling emotionally drained or down at the time, I have the choice to say no, and ask that we talk at a later date. That empowers and strengthens our friendship in a way that builds trust and openness between us.

The other tool to use here is offering feedback in a way that puts the onus on the person giving the feedback, rather than blaming the person we are speaking to, making ourselves wrong, not them. For example, if someone does something we thought we'd asked them not to do, we can say, "Apparently I didn't explain this to you properly…" In this way, we can use the tool to enhance our own skills of clear communication.

Whenever possible I like to use the "sandwich" technique when I am communicating feedback. I sandwich the feedback between two compliments or statements of appreciation. For example, I am receiving a massage and the therapist is not quite hitting the spot I want. I may say, "I really love what you are doing, but I'd like you to go a little deeper around the scapula, please." Then, when they do what I requested, I can say, "Thank you. That feels really great." In this way I get my needs met and the therapist feels validated.

Our inner critic…

We are all familiar with the voice in our head that gets on our case, that criticizes and judges us for not being good enough, smart enough, compassionate enough, spiritual enough, and so on. Like the last chapter where we talked about our inner judge, here too the invitation is to use our witness to observe when the inner critic is active and acknowledge it. A nice tool to use here is to enlist the help of another character in our heads, our inner advocate. The advocate is the good guy who is on our side, who builds us up and says nice things about us, at the same time encouraging our growth and self-improvement. In this way, we can have a dialog running between the two parts of ourselves.

For example, we feel like having a massage and money is tight. Our inner critic is telling us that we are selfish and mean and that money could be better spent on things for the kids. Then our inner advocate speaks up and says yes, but we work hard for our money and deserve to get pampered occasionally and honor ourselves in this way. My inner advocate is like a cartoon character of Miss Piggy. She is feisty and out-spoken on my behalf and has no problem honoring the little girl inside of me who wants to go and eat ice cream once in a while. My witness observes these conversations in my head and in this way I find that the technique helps me to balance my mind and dissipate the negative energy of my self-judgment.

Eventually...

Our inner critic can gradually become our ally, helping us to be discerning instead of judgmental. As we continue our spiritual path, criticism fades away more and more. Instead, we just accept everything as it is, unless we are asked for feedback, in which case we respond appropriately.

> *"Never criticize a man until you have walked a mile in his moccasins."*
> —Ancient Native American saying.

Examples:

My friend owns his own company and can be quite demanding of his staff. One day his assistant failed to write an important letter in the way he had wanted, and mailed the letter out before he approved it. He was furious and yelled and screamed at the girl, blaming and criticizing her for not doing as he had asked.

Instead, he could have communicated like this: "I'm so sorry that I didn't communicate with you clearly enough as to how to write this letter and our procedure for mail-outs. Now for the future, can you tell me how I can ensure that we understand each other concerning mail that goes out so that this doesn't happen again?"

My ex-boyfriend was very critical of my cooking. It's not my strong point but I do try! Once he said, "This soup tastes awful. It's bland and uninteresting." I felt like pouring it on him. Maybe he could have spoken his truth in a gentler way like this: "Thank you for going to so much trouble making the soup. Can I give you some feedback on how it was for me and share my personal taste with you? Next time maybe we could add a few more herbs for flavor." That would have been a loving criticism that would have left me feeling appreciated and only too pleased for the suggestion.

Performance evaluations in the workplace are opportunities to get honest feedback from your supervisor as to how you are doing your job. In this instance, there is an implied agreement about the feedback. You know it is coming! However, here again it is important to filter out the agenda of your supervisor and take in the feedback that is really meaningful for you.

My friend Jacqueline has parents who have always been very critical of her. One day when she was talking to her mom on the telephone and her mom was letting loose the usual barrage of criticism, Jacqueline said, "Mom, I get it that you really love me and care about me." There was nothing more that needed to be said. That was the truth, and instead of getting defensive and engaging with her mother over the details of life, Jacqueline just acknowledged the deeper level of what was going on.

> *The path says, "I've never met a man so stupid I could not learn something from or one so smart I could not teach something to."*

Exercises:

Immediate action:

Watch your tendency to criticize others. Play with turning the criticism into positive feedback and asking for permission to share first.

Engage the help of the inner advocate whenever the inner critic shows up!

Ongoing awareness:

Notice how it feels to be criticized, as opposed to receiving feedback. Start to let the person know if the criticism hurt you in any way and if there was a different way they could have shared their opinions with you.

A saint ran across one of his ex-students one day. This person began to vilify the saint, calling her all kinds of names and unleashing all his anger at her. The saint listened to the man, then looked at him and asked, "What happens if you give someone a gift and the person refuses to accept the gift?"

"Well, you get to keep the gift," replied the man.

"And I am refusing your gift," said the saint, and walked away.

CLEARING UP THE PAST

There is a dark shadow that haunts our present—it's called our past.

Unless we can release ourselves from the emotional hooks that trigger our behavior we cannot truly be present in the moment. These emotional hooks will run us and we will react according to engrained behavior patterns that are lodged deep within our cellular memory.

We spend our childhood laying these patterns down. As conscious adults, we spend our adult years unraveling and releasing them so we can be empty inside, ready and willing to respond appropriately without the trigger of the past to color our behavior.

The process of unraveling is often a lifetime's work. The tools offered in the following chapters are a gentle way to facilitate this process. We work on releasing shame and guilt, unburdening our secrets, practicing complete forgiveness, and letting go of objects from the past that tie us to old energy. Once we have completed this unfinished business we can be more available for our lives in the present.

9

Who do I need to forgive?

Heals our relationships and ourselves

Withholding forgiveness causes us to suffer. When we can't forgive there can be no intimacy, no love. That's an expensive price to pay! To forgive is to set a prisoner free and discover that we were the prisoner!

When we think that someone wronged us and we bear that person a grudge, we are wasting our precious energy. It takes energy to hold on tightly to that grudge, even if we are not aware of it, and that holding on weighs us down energetically. A friend of mine likes to use the expression that anyone she hasn't been able to forgive is occupying rent-free space in her mind!

We need to release the idea that the past can improve. What happened, happened, and the only thing that we have the power to change is the present, that is, our perceptions and behavior that are going on right now. Not forgiving on some level keeps us stuck in the past, hooked into the events that caused our anguish, and even attracting similar situations to us until we can get the lesson to forgive and move on.

As long as we hold other people responsible for our unhappiness, we are adopting the position of victim and refusing to admit responsibility for our life. Having the attitude that "they did it to me" and blaming others never makes us happy or moves us forward. It's just an excuse not to take action to change something we are unhappy with.

When we let go of our grudges, we get to let go of the resentment and blame. We release the baggage of the experience.

What happens is a lightening up, an energy dynamic that helps us to feel clearer and less burdened. This frees us up to be more present and appropriate in the moment without letting the past trigger our emotions.

Owning our shadow...

Forgiveness is 100% or nothing. We can't half forgive someone. Saying, "I forgive you" is not the same as feeling forgiveness in our heart and experiencing the release of forgiveness at a cellular level. We will know when we have been successful because there will no longer be an emotional charge for us around that person. No more will we start clenching our jaw and gnashing our teeth when we hear the perpetrator's name!

So how do we get to a place of 100% forgiveness? There is one really solid tool that I have found to help us here. It relates to the practice of "owning our shadow," as Carl Gustav Jung, the famed Swiss psychologist, would say.

We are all human, and as part of our human make-up we have the capacity for love, generosity, truth, kindness, and charity. We are also capable of hatred, meanness, sloth, lying, and cheating. Each and every one of us! These "negative" traits are what make up our shadow side, the part of ourselves that we do our best to hide from the rest of the world. As we mature, we do our best to be "good" people and live sweetly in society in a way that promotes harmony and peace rather then conflict and mistrust. However, the value of digging deep inside ourselves and looking at all aspects of our fundamental human nature is that we discover that we too have the capacity to do "evil" things, even though we may choose not to. With regard to forgiveness, if we can get it that we too have the capacity to do the wrong that we think was done to us, then we can feel some true compassion for the person who has wronged us and can finally get to a place of true forgiveness.

Jesus illustrated this pretty well when a prostitute was about to be stoned to death and he shouted out to the crowd, "He who is without sin, cast the first stone!" Her life was saved as everyone realized they had all had lapses of expressing their darker side at times. No one is 100% lily-white!

There is a famous saying, "There but for the Grace of God go I." We can take a moment to imagine what it must be like to be that person, to stand in their shoes and to feel what they feel. In truth, everyone is doing the best they can with the tools they have. If it is hard to forgive someone, try seeing that person's mistake as a deviation from their natural place of love and innocence. So it's not about what a bad person they are, but about their need to heal their own wounds. Forgiving them and holding them in their highest light can help them in their healing process so that a new context of behavior can occur.

When we can't forgive...

There is also another way to look at this. Imagine we are angels in heaven. You are an angel who wants to learn forgiveness. But in order to learn forgiveness you have to have something to forgive. So you make a deal with an angel friend that during your next incarnation on earth, they will do something to you so terrible that you will be in a position to have a choice as to whether to forgive or bear a grudge. Your angel friend agrees to do this from a place of love, but reminds you that when you are on the earth you may forget this agreement and it may be very hard for you to forgive at that time. And that is the point—if forgiveness were easy it would have no value and would hold no growth for us as souls. Seen in this light, the people we interact with who harm us in some way offer us an enormous potential for growth and love. Indeed, we can be grateful for their presence in our lives once we understand this.

> *The saint who got stabbed said to his killer as he was dying, "You can't fool me—I see God in you too."*

Forgiving our parents...

We can never truly be healthy adults until we have healed the relationship with our parents. They were our primary relationship, and how we feel about them colors our relationships with all other people on an unconscious level. It is not about what they did or didn't do to us as kids, it's about how we feel about what they did. So even if our parents are dead, we can still work on ourselves in order to clear any resentment we may have towards them.

Early childhood trauma becomes a drama in adult life unless it is mourned and healed. We need to remember our abuses and neglect, feel the emotions of sadness and fear that surround them, re-run the events in our mind which have the greatest charge for us, and say what needs expressing, using the clearing techniques outlined below. I suggest scanning through the childhood years, from 0–5, 5–10, 10–15, etc. to see which incidents light up for us as we think back in time.

Once we have expressed ourselves fully, we can look for what was learned and gained from the experience and be grateful for those lessons. With this new awareness we can finally forgive our parents for the part they played in our personal movie of life.

Clearing at a cellular level...

Practicing forgiveness and releasing its burden on us sometimes requires more than just saying, "I forgive you." If there has been a deep-seated grudge or resentment, then I suggest the following technique. Lie or sit down comfortably and close the eyes. See the person you want to forgive in front of your mind's eye. Either silently or out loud express to them the feelings you had around the incident. Be truthful. Do not withhold anything. If tears or other emotions arise, do not try to stop them. This is the chance they have been waiting for to release out of your system, where they have been suppressed for so long.

When you have had your say, listen for the person's response. If we can accept the fact that on a deep quantum level we are all connected, doing this exercise can allow some real communication and healing to occur. Be open to hearing what this person has to say to you, even if you think you are imagining it all, and then respond again.

Continue the dialogue until it feels complete. Then do to the person whatever it feels right to do—it could be you want to give them a hug, or it could be you want to send them into outer space.

Do whatever feels good to you so that you feel complete with this process and can forgive them completely. Then begin to take some deep breaths. Imagine that the grudge/resentment has a color. Look inside and see where it is hiding in the body, and as you breathe, begin to gather up this color into a colorful mass, and when you have it all, send it up into the atmosphere in a big balloon to be cleansed and cleared by the atmosphere and the angels. Then breathe in golden light energy from a cloud that sits right above your head, to fill up the spaces where the resentment was being held. Do this until you feel clear and uplifted.

Another technique is to use "I release" statements. For example, "I release any guilt I had been harboring around teasing my little sister when I was a kid." This can be nicely followed with a simple ritual to symbolize the release. For example, light a candle and after the release statement blow it out.

> *"The weak can never forgive. Forgiveness is an attribute of the strong."* —Mahatma Gandhi

Forgiving ourselves...

Often we are hardest on ourselves. We beat ourselves up for all kinds of reasons—not fulfilling expectations, not being "good enough," feeling guilty, and many other such things. When we forgive ourselves, we can let go of guilt and remorse. Why continue to punish ourselves for what we perceive as our own shortcomings? It's only a belief system that does not serve us. We need to get it that we did the best we could at the time, we didn't do anything wrong, but rather we had the opportunity to learn valuable lessons from our behavior.

We can ask ourselves if there is anyone that we feel we have wronged and would like to make amends to. If we are carrying a burden of guilt for something that happened in the past, we can ask to be released from it. We can invite the person whom we feel we wronged to speak their truth to us about the incident. We can be surrendered, vulnerable, and available to them as we listen to what they have to say. Their words will often surprise us. Even if we do not hold this conversation with them in person, but rather, by imagining them here with us, the effect is the same. After we have completed this conversation, we can say to ourselves verbally, "I forgive you," and welcome our younger, previously ostracized self back into our heart.

Eventually…

The need for forgiveness starts to fall away as we clean our lives up and get more conscious. Needing to forgive implies that we have judged someone for something bad that they did to us, or judged ourselves. The more we take responsibility for our lives, the more we can understand that there is really nothing ever to forgive! Everything in our lives shows up for a reason and is there for our learning and growth. All we need to do is to pay attention to it and be grateful, accepting all situations as they occur in the moment.

> *"Blaming the weather never helped anybody. The same goes for blaming other people. When we do choose to forgive, a marvelous principle comes into operation. As we change, others change. As we alter our attitude toward others, they begin to alter their behavior. Somehow, the moment we choose to change the way we see things, others respond to our changed expectations."*
> —Andrew Matthews, *Being Happy*

Examples:

Joanne could not forgive her sister for stealing a boyfriend of hers when she was sixteen. Since then there had always been a strange feeling between them, a lack of trust, a lack of intimacy. It wasn't until Joanne's sister was getting married that Joanne finally decided to bury the hatchet. She talked to her sister, admitted that she had been carrying that incident with her and shared that she was now ready to forgive and let it go. Only then were they able to be close as sisters once more.

A friend of mine once had an affair with a man who had recently left his wife. The affair was short-lived, yet during that time she would receive phone calls from the wife, who even threatened suicide. Eventually her lover returned to be with his wife. My friend carried the guilt of her pain for many years. One day she saw the wife at a resort. She introduced herself and apologized for her part in causing so much pain all those years ago. She forgave her, they hugged, and a great weight was lifted from her life.

Another friend of mine was severely abused by an elder brother as a child and adolescent, both physically and emotionally. This brother could beat his body but never his spirit. Now my friend realizes the gift in the beatings was that he grew stronger and more independent as a result. This has stood him in good stead in later life. He says now there is nothing to forgive his brother for. It was just as it needed to be for his unfoldment.

> *"Forgiveness is the mental technique by which our thoughts are transformed from fear to love."*
> —Marianne Williamson, *Return to Love*

Exercises:

Immediate action:

Take a forgiveness inventory. On one sheet of paper, write down the things you feel you need to forgive yourself for—anything you feel guilty about or have judged yourself for. Recall what you learned from that experience. Next cut the paper into pieces and for every act of forgiveness, acknowledge that you did the best that you could at the time, offer a prayer of release to God, and let your feelings of guilt burn up with the paper in a candle flame.

On another sheet, write down the names of people about whom you are resentful. Next to their name, write down what you learned from the interaction.

Follow-up: If you feel it is necessary, have a conversation with those people whom you wish to forgive and let them know that you no longer hold a grudge. Do the cellular clearing exercise described earlier as many times as necessary.

Ongoing awareness:

Clear the air continually with those whom you feel you have wronged or who you feel have wronged you. Be available to listen to what they have to say to you. As you do this, check in with yourself to make sure you have released any lingering guilt or resentment you may be carrying.

There were once two monks who became prisoners of war. During their capture they were treated quite brutally and with great cruelty. Eventually, the war ended and they were released. The monks were interviewed by a journalist, who asked them if they could forgive their captors for their rough treatment. The first monk said, "Absolutely not! I shall never be able to forgive those prison guards!" To which the second monk replied, "Then you are still in prison!"

10

Can I bring myself current?

Releases us from the shackles of the past

Many of us are attached to our past out of habit. We hang on to stuff that no longer serves us—clothes that used to fit, our ex-husband's furniture, and attitudes and behaviors that are hooked into our past conditioning. Bringing ourselves current involves examining aspects of our lives such as our external surroundings or habitual behaviors to see if they reflect who we are now or what we wish to become.

Clearing our environment...

We've all heard the old adage, "Cleanliness is next to godliness." Doesn't it feel just really good to have a clean, tidy house where everything works and we know exactly where everything is? On some level, that frees our energy so we can be more ourselves. We can fix the broken things in the house, throw away anything that is just collecting dust, and get rid of clutter. This is the principle behind Feng Shui, that when we change the energy in our environment, we change the energy in our life.

I have a friend who is often depressed. She says that when she is feeling down, her house is a mess and she has no motivation to tidy up. Conversely, when the house is tidy, she is less likely to fall into a depression, as she feels she is the master of her environment and this empowers her.

Like my depressed friend, I have noticed that people who live in untidy, cluttered houses are not as capable of moving through blocks in their lives. They feel more stuck, not as empowered to meet their challenges. It's also very hard for them to take that step and start getting rid of the clutter. The inner is a reflection of the outer.

The good news is that if we can start to deal with our immediate environment on the external level, it will be easier for us to move forward with our inner growth, too. Therefore if we feel life is stagnating for us, we can look to see how we can rid ourselves of stagnation in our environment first, and watch the energy in the rest of our life begin to shift. We can begin by doing simple things like sorting out old photos, having a garage sale, and deleting old files on the computer!

Of course there will be some things that need to go in the garbage, but there will also be things that we can give away to a new home to be loved anew. There are plenty of charity organizations that are only too happy to receive old furniture, clothing or housewares. Sometimes my girlfriends and I get together and do a clothing, CD, and book swap! We bring all our unwanted music, books, and clothes and put them in a big pile in the middle of the room and just take what we want! Whatever is left, we donate to a charity shop. It's such a fun thing to do and it really helps everybody. Another nice technique to help us unload formerly precious and sentimental objects is to bless and thank those things that have served us well. Then we can release them with a sense of sacredness and honor. I have a girlfriend who took her old wedding ring to the sea and conducted her own private ceremony of reflecting on her marriage and all it taught her, before throwing the ring into the sea as a symbol of release.

Friendships...

Let's look at friendships. Do the people in our life reflect the person we are today, or do we need a new circle of friends? People grow and evolve at different rates. The friend we grew up with in high school may no longer resonate with us today. Sometimes we need to move on and leave some friendships behind. We can still care deeply for that person without having to spend time with them repeating the same old patterns.

One of my students, Vicki, used to go out regularly with her old boss and their respective spouses. After a while, she started to notice that she was no longer enjoying their outings. Her old boss had a tendency to be negative and critical, whereas Vicki works hard on her self-awareness, practicing gratitude and observing closely her thoughts and feelings. After their last outing, the old boss said that Vicki should plan the next one. Vicki in her heart was done with the relationship, and had no intention of spending more time with this woman in the same way. Her dilemma was how to end the friendship without hurting her friend's feelings but staying in her own integrity.

She decided that she would do nothing, and would wait for the lady to call her again. When she did, Vicki told her that she was focusing on spiritual growth and spending time with people who were on a similar journey. As her time was precious, she was no longer going to go on purely social evenings. Instead, she suggested that the lady join her at one of our jnana yoga groups, making it clear that only in that type of arena was she prepared to spend time with her. Vicki spoke her truth of where she was at, without having to attack or criticize her friend. She gave her friend the option of moving in this direction with her or not. The friend chose not to.

Getting closure...

An extremely valuable exercise is to look at our close relationships and see what kind of closure or completion is necessary with these people. Pretend the world is going to end next week—what is it we would need to say or do to bring ourselves truly current with them? Think about words of love and appreciation, that so often do not get expressed. When did we last thank our parents for putting up with us for eighteen years while we were kids? Or appreciate our siblings for something nice they said to us once, when we were feeling down, that really helped us feel good about ourselves? Have we thanked our best friend for being there for us when we needed to talk? The work we talked about in the forgiveness chapter is pertinent here, too—making amends, forgiving, and moving forward. Have we spoken our truth to all the people who need to hear it?

It is really empowering for us to complete all our unfinished business with people in the material sense, too. We need to take inventory of what this means for us—for example, by making good on promises and agreements, paying debts, or returning books we have borrowed. We also need to deal with people who have unfinished business with us, reminding them to do their part in tying up any loose ends. Suggesting timelines for this completion can be helpful here, so we can complete our business in a timely way. When we have unfinished business, there is an energy leak that keeps us invested in our past. Cleaning up our lives brings us current so we have more energy available for our present.

Personal care...

Do you still have the same hairstyle you wore as a teenager? Look at yourself closely in the mirror. Who is this person? Do your clothes reflect who you are, or are you still wearing hand-me-downs from your big sister or brother? This is the time to attack the depths of the closet! Give away anything you haven't worn for the past year—be ruthless here! Go through your old sock drawer, throwing out the old socks that never found their pairs. Are you still waiting for afghan coats to come back into fashion? There's a retro 60's store in your town that would probably love to have that coat!

Look at eating habits. Many people eat the way their family of origin did, without questioning whether different eating habits may serve them better. Sometimes a little experimentation is in order so we can have a direct experience of what works for us now, in the body we have today. My family always ate cereal for breakfast laden with sugar. As I have grown older I have noticed that my body does not tolerate wheat and sugar very well. Now I drink a smoothie each morning with high-quality protein powder, organic fruits, and yogurt to give my body the nutrition it needs.

Attitudes and behavior...

We often take on our parents' attitudes and the attitudes of peer groups, teachers, and friends without consciously realizing it. Where do our belief systems come from anyway? Are they coming from our past environment or from our own experience? It's important here to bring our attention to present time by re-examining where we stand on issues today, as the person we now are.

When I lived in England I always used to vote for the Conservative Party because that's who my family voted for. I did this without taking the time to understand the political issues at stake. Similarly, prejudices are often inherited from our families. We hear them and parrot them off, often for many years, without examining what is true for us. When I worked in London, I lived in Brixton, home to many West Indian people. Some of my friends and family could not believe that I would choose to live there. "Aren't you afraid you'll be mugged?" "How can you walk home alone late at night and not be frightened?" Well, I lived there for three years and had nothing but good experiences with the locals in the area. I had no fear of them and they were always friendly towards me.

We also absorb behavior patterns from those around us. Sometimes this results in funny stories. My mother always cut the turkey in half when she put it in the oven at Christmas. Someone once asked her why. She replied, "This is the way my mother always did it, and it always turned out great." Then one year her mother came for Christmas dinner and watched with horror as her daughter cut the turkey in half before she put it in the oven.

"Why are you doing that?" she asked.

"Because you always did," my mother replied.

"But I had to," my grandmother replied. "You see, our oven wasn't big enough for it to go in any other way!"

Examples:

Robert's father is a cowboy. He brought up Robert to rope steer, shoot deer, and fish. When I met him, his house was full of relics of his past such as guns and deer heads complete with antlers. But this no longer reflected the person he had become—a vegetarian who no longer killed animals, and who was on a dedicated spiritual path. Robert began to let go of his past. He sold his guns, burned his photos, and gave away his antlers. His experience was that this created a living space far more able to support the person he now was. The energy in his house felt completely different—much softer, and a good environment for meditation and spiritual practice.

As part of a jnana yoga exercise, I wrote to my parents, stepmother, and grandmother a letter of appreciation. In each letter I thanked them for being in my life and for all the wonderful things they have done for me over the years. It felt really good to me to write those letters, and that was the point. What they did with them was none of my business. However, I do remember receiving a phone call from my mother with tears in her voice, saying she had proudly read the letter to her office colleagues and that she would treasure it forever!

My friend Herb has always loved cars. He has two classic cars in his garage and another in his driveway. He rarely drives them, but has always proudly held onto them. He recently has been working on bringing himself current, and realized that his past was somehow tied up in those cars—the vigor of his youth, the person he used to be, and all that nostalgia. He finally got rid of two of the cars and reported that he felt so much freer and more able to be who he is now without the weight of the past, exemplified by those cars dragging on him.

Exercises:

Immediate action:

Look around you and see what it is you could let go of that would serve you to do so. Clean out the house/closet/car.

And/or: Write a letter of appreciation to someone you love.

Ongoing awareness:

Bring your relationships current. Examine your friendships, the company you keep. Do the people you choose to spend time with reflect who you are and support you in your life-path? Look to see with whom you spend your energy. Does it serve either of you? Or is this an old habit pattern?

Ongoing nightly practice: At the end of each day when you go to bed, spend some quiet time reflecting on your day. Notice anything that came up during the day that disturbed your peace. Maybe you have judged yourself or others, or you did something you feel guilty about. Whatever it is, feel it again, embrace it as part of your day's experience, and offer it up to the Divine as just that, releasing the charge that the incident carried with it. If you feel it necessary, ask forgiveness from God. This practice will keep you current with emotional baggage as you release it on a daily basis.

There was a soldier in the Vietnam war who was captured by the Viet Kong. He was placed in a solitary cell. Every day he was taken from his cell and beaten, sometimes so badly that he could no longer walk.

To keep his spirit alive he decided to make a practice of remembering his life so far in every last detail, from his earliest childhood to the present day. As he went through this process day after day, his heart swelled with gratitude and love for the friends and family in his life. He forgave those who had wronged him and he found compassion for himself as he recalled learning so many of life's lessons the hard way.

As he brought himself current with this practice of remembering he found his heart filling more and more with love, for life, for the people in his past and eventually even for those soldiers who were beating him. When the guards took him out each day to give him his daily beating he could do nothing but beam up at them, sending them waves of love. He no longer resisted the beatings. He surrendered completely to his fate. After a while his captors no longer knew what to do with him, so they let him go. (This is a true story.)

11

What's the secret?

Frees us from our shame

How many of us are prisoners in our own minds of deep, dark secrets, the content of which we are sure would make everyone hate us if they only knew? How many of us really have the courage to be vulnerable, remove our masks, and confess our shame, our guilt, our deepest fears, and our negative emotions? When we hold a secret inside, it feels so big, so heavy. But when we let it out to the universe, the simple act of sharing it with others has the effect of lightening our load.

When a secret is shared it is by definition no longer a secret. It can no longer hold power over us. Experience often tells us that when we do allow ourselves to become vulnerable and share our innermost thoughts with our friends, therapists, or ministers, that not only do we relieve ourselves of this burden of having a secret, but it also goes a long way towards deepening our friendships. When we share our secrets and reveal our shame we are demonstrating that we trust our friends. This creates intimacy. How far along the path of intimacy and friendship are we willing to tread?

Taking the risk to be vulnerable...

This is particularly important as regards our partners in life. If we withhold secrets from our partners we can have no true intimacy. Besides, what is it your beloved could possibly say to you about anything that happened in the past that would change your love for them right now in this moment? If you cannot accept your partner just the way they are, no matter what they may have done before, the love is limited.

Sharing our secrets takes courage. We take the risk that the person we share our secrets with may judge us harshly and no longer love us. We need to pick our confessor with discernment. We need to feel that whatever our secrets are, they will be gently accepted, without criticism or melodrama. It is important to be able to share our secrets with people who will not judge us in any way. After all, we've probably judged ourselves pretty thoroughly as it is.

The issue is in the tissue...

There may be secrets stored in our cellular memory that we are not even aware of. Often when we are traumatized as children, we consciously "forget" the trauma, as it is just too much for us to handle when we are young. But the memory of it is stored in our tissues, sometimes creating tightness in parts of the body or even health challenges. It's almost as if the body stores the emotions around traumatic events until we are really ready and equipped to deal with them. Massage practitioners and body-workers often find that during sessions their clients begin to remember previously hidden memories as the tissues where the memories were stored get massaged and manipulated. This can happen in hatha yoga classes also. We experience the trauma going into our body and we experience the trauma as it leaves. Sometimes the actual memory will become clear. Other times it will be a nonspecific release of anger, grief, or sadness. Either way it is a part of our healing process and is a necessary part of our life's journey.

Toxic shame...

Shame is a created emotion. It is simply a reaction to other people's judgments. It's the illusion that there is something we can do that is wrong and there's no possibility of forgiveness, no matter how much we say "I'm sorry." When the garbage truck of shame is dumped upon us we contract and lose our sense of power. We think we have been "bad" and there's nothing we can do about it. Its burden weighs heavily upon our psyche, running our lives in ways we are often not aware of until we take the time to delve into our past and dredge up our moments of shame for re-investigation.

Shame is a controlling device. People shame their children in order to have more control over them. "You should be ashamed of yourself!" they may say to the child. The more defiant and powerful the child and the more threatened the parent, the more the likelihood of shaming devices being used to control the child. Similarly, husbands shame their wives and wives shame their husbands. Religious leaders shame their congregation. The amount of shame is often proportional to the degree of fear and need for control of the perpetrator.

Shame has a huge destructive potential. Not only does it disempower us as individuals, but when we have been shamed we are capable of passing it on to others unless we consciously break the pattern. Hate crimes are rooted in our unhealed burden of shame. Nazi Germany enrolled whole populations to carry out atrocities as they came out of their shame from World War One.

Healing our shame...

The first step towards healing our shame is to recognize those moments in our lives when we felt shamed, and feel once again what that was like for us. Shame was designed to demobilize us. Now we need to give ourselves permission to feel it, know it, and move it through. This will often lead to grief and sadness, because we are no longer imprisoned in our web of shame and can now feel fully the emotions that it hid.

It is also vitally important to release the energy of our shame from our cellular memory in order to be completely free of it. We need to meditate on where we stored our feelings of shame in our physical or energy body and consciously breathe into those places, releasing that old energy out of our body with breath and intention. The best way to do this is to share our shame with other people who accept us and can hear us without judgment—for example, a hypnotherapist or counselor who can help guide us through our process of release, or a support group that deals with these types of issues. That way we can feel supported in our process, which will aid us in our healing.

For the past nine years I have belonged to a women's group

in Sacramento that meets every two weeks to work on spiritual development. From time to time we close the group so we can develop a circle of intimacy and trust and share at a very deep level. In this group I have had the courage to share some of my darkest secrets and most "shameful" behaviors with the ladies that could have given them lots of reason to judge me. However, in this group when I have told the ladies my secrets, all I have had reflected back is acceptance and love for me just the way I am. It has been such a healing experience for me, and such a great opportunity to let go of my secrets without fear of judgment. I highly recommend joining such a group or starting your own!

Owning our shadow side...

As mentioned in the chapter on forgiveness, we all have our dark side, the part of our personality that conjures up evil thoughts and has the capacity to be selfish, lazy, and greedy, and to lie, cheat, and steal. We've all wanted to harm someone at some time or other—even if it was only a fleeting thought. Indeed, as human beings we all have the potential to be a Hitler or a Mother Teresa.

Naturally, most of us want to be good citizens and gravitate towards nurturing the more positive aspects of our personality. Our shadow side exists within us nonetheless and if ignored can run amok at inconvenient times. What if we could embrace our shadow, knowing that it's what makes us human beings, and let that be a path towards becoming more whole and accepting ourselves more fully? What if we could confess our darkest feelings of anger, lust, jealousy and greed to others, giving these feelings a voice before they erupt uncontrolled, causing havoc in our lives? We cannot become fully powerful without owning all of our parts, and we cut off our creative flow when we do not acknowledge our negative personality. Here again, talking about our shadow thoughts and feelings with friends or counselors can be an excellent way of moving the energy that is behind the thoughts and feelings.

I have always been one to ignore my dark side. I wanted to be "nice," kind and sweet. It wasn't until I entered my forties that I began to see the price I paid for not revealing all parts of my true nature. It cost me intimacy in relationships. It cost me my personal power. And it kept me stuck in low self-esteem. After much soul-searching, I am now no longer afraid to say when I am angry about something, or feeling frustrated or just plain depressed. I no longer have to keep up this façade of perfection. The result is that I can now show up more fully in relationships. My partner no longer has to dig to find out how I am really feeling. I no longer keep it a secret!

> *True peace and serenity are tempered in the fires of adversity.*

Examples:

When I was seven years old, we had team netball competitions at school. Being fiercely competitive at that young age, I really wanted my team to win. So when the other team whom I saw as our main competition shot a goal, I booed them. The games teacher came over to all of us standing watching the match. I can hear her words still so clearly. "Who booed?" she asked, with an angry look in her eye. And again, "Who booed?" I was too ashamed to own up—I was afraid of looking foolish in the eyes of both my teacher and my schoolmates. So the games were stopped and the whole school was sent inside instead. I carried that shame with me for many years.

I recently led a workshop called "Healing Feminine Shame." I thought I had dredged up all of my sexual and adolescent shame in previous sessions. To my surprise, when I invited the group to meditate on shameful moments from their lives, another memory popped into my head that I had completely forgotten about. When I was five years old I had started school. The first week I was there, I peed in my pants during school assembly. I remember the teacher took all of us out one by one and felt us to see if we were wet. Of course I was. I nearly fainted with embarrassment. My teacher gave me a scolding that I will never forget. Through the group process I became aware that I was carrying shame around this incident, too, that needed to be released.

My friends Kriya and John began their relationship by sharing every dark secret they could possibly think of with each other. They have a commitment to not have any secrets from each other at all. They say this agreement has strengthened their bond of trust and level of intimacy greatly.

Exercises:

Specific exercise:

We all have secrets. Write down those that you have never confessed to anyone and begin the process of sharing them. Start with the easier ones, maybe sharing with close friends. Or if it is too hard to say it out loud, write down your secret and hand it to your friend for reading. Choose your confessor wisely, someone non-judgmental and trustworthy. Or go to a professional therapist. See how it feels to unburden yourself. Notice the fear come up that you will be judged. However, with a true friend there is nothing that you can say or do that will change the way that friend feels about you.

Offer to be your friend's confessor also. Give the gift of listening without judgment, listening with love's ear. Just be receptive of their trust in you.

Ongoing awareness:

Start to meditate on events in your life that have caused you to feel shame. Confess them to a trusted friend. Be aware of where those feelings are held in the body and begin a process to release them. Notice how differently you feel about yourself as you let go of your burden of shame.

There was once a great Tibetan Saint called Milarepa. He was meditating in a cave one night when 3 demons came to haunt him. "Wooooohhhh," they wailed. "We are big and scary and we have come to torment you." The demons made frightening-looking shadows on the wall of the cave and continued to utter menacing sounds.

"Who are you?" asked Milarepa calmly.

"I am the demon of shame," replied one. "I am the demon of fear," replied another. "And I am the demon of guilt," said the third.

Recognizing pieces of his own shadow in each of them, Milarepa said, "Well, then come in and have a cup of tea with me."

IN EACH MOMENT

Mindfulness, that is, the practice of staying conscious and aware in everyday life, has long been a tradition of Zen Buddhists as well as the yogis. Modern day living places stresses and demands on us that make this practice even more relevant today. We can use the techniques of mindfulness to take a moment, slow down, see what's necessary, and come from a place of love.

12

What would love do now?

Transforms our relationships with ourselves and others

Our primary purpose for being alive is to share love. Can we be in the world in such a way that our every thought, word, and deed reflect our true nature as beings of love with regard to ourselves, other people, the environment, our community, and God? How can we keep our hearts open so as to let our love out and let in the love of the people in our lives? The challenge is to tear down the walls that encase our hearts so we can be vulnerable and available, sensitive to ourselves and others.

Loving ourselves...

The yogis say that the only thing that God wants from us is for us to be a well-loved being. Indeed, this is probably the most challenging, yet important, life work that each of us gets to explore. Being well-loved is not about how many other people love us but about what we are doing to take care of ourselves. The irony is, the more we take responsibility for loving ourselves, the more we draw love from others into our lives. Indeed, our capacity for loving others is directly related to our capacity for self-love. The effect snowballs until we are brimming over with love, just the way God wants it!

So what does this look like on a practical level? First and foremost, we love ourselves by accepting ourselves fully, just the way we are, with all our perceived imperfections. When we do, we know intrinsically that our presence in the world is enough. That is, in order to be valuable in the world, there is nothing we need do except be present and conscious. This gives us the foundation for self-esteem, which in turn helps us to do things on a day-to-day basis to take good care of ourselves, because we know we are worth it.

Loving ourselves means making choices we can be proud of, choices that empower and nurture us. For example, we can look after the body, eating healthier food and doing more exercise, honor ourselves as much as possible by working at a job that brings us joy, spend time with people who feed our spirit, take time out to just have fun, notice where the abuse occurs in our life and take steps to cut it out, or know when to say "no" to extra commitments. There are an infinite number of ways for us to love ourselves, and no-one else can do it as well as we can!

In our Sacramento jnana yoga group we recently did two exercises around this theme. One was to make a list of all the things we do to love, honor, and nurture the self, and the other was to make a list of all the things we can do to raise our energetic vibration. The lists ended up being almost identical! It became clear to us that loving ourselves does raise our vibration, which is most helpful for our spiritual development, our sensitivity, and our energy. Here are some of the things that we wrote down:

being in nature
asking for support
being in integrity
taking a hot bath
playing music
singing
writing in our journal
deep breathing
hatha yoga
curling up in bed for a nap
preparing delicious food
art
being with animals
hugging
completing a task
gardening
cleaning
walking

massage
doing something that makes us laugh
watching uplifting movies
dancing
meditation
prayer

It can be helpful to copy this list and refer to it whenever we need a lift. Add some things to it that give you joy too!

My friend Jan uses the technique of "treating herself like she was three!" to love herself more. For her this means not breaking promises or commitments to herself, giving herself credit, being confident and trusting in her path, not judging herself or beating herself up, not expecting perfection, and dialoguing with her inner child to make sure her needs are being honored. It might occasionally mean buying herself an ice-cream as a treat as well! We tend to treat other people so much better than we do ourselves, so it's a wonderful practice to offer ourselves the same gentleness and kindness as we would a small child.

> *"You can travel the whole world and never find anyone more deserving of love than you."*
> —The Buddha

Loving others...

One way to love others is to be as present as possible, really hearing what is being communicated, without judging or reacting from a place of ego. We can call this "listening with love's ear." Everyone wants to be heard and acknowledged, but so rarely do we take the time to listen to each other without agenda. Rather, we listen through a screen of resistance, made up of our prejudices, our daily worries, desires, and fears, so when we listen we are really only hearing our own noise, and not what is being said. Instead, we can consciously empty ourselves of our inner noise and have the experience of the presence of listening, hearing the other person without the need to comment or offer our opinions, except when asked. This helps us to be in a receptive state of mind where things can be more easily understood. We can even hear behind the words, to what is really being communicated.

Listening to others is one of the greatest gifts we can give. It is a skill that has the power to transform our relationships, especially if we can learn to listen with an open heart. However, this does not mean that we let people dump all their issues and melodramas on us, needlessly sucking our energy and attention as they do so! Adding the element of loving ourselves requires that we learn to say "Stop" to people who insist on repeating the same old stories again and again. Let's not forget to listen to ourselves with love's ears as well, to ensure that our own inner voice is being honored!

Love shares... and we establish intimacy when we share deeply of ourselves, expressing our thoughts, feelings and experiences. When someone asks how we are, how do we reply? Are we always "just fine" or do we take the time to tell the person what is really going on for us? If we always hold back and never share of our deepest self, either because we feel we are not worthy to be listened to or we will be judged as weak in some way, then the gateway to our heart is closed and no-one can reach out to us. Instead, by taking the risk to be vulnerable and trusting the person with our inner feelings and thoughts, we invite the possibility for true communion with another, which opens the door to the experience of love.

Speaking our truth to others and sharing our feelings in a sensitive, appropriate way is a powerful way to demonstrate our love and caring. We can call this "speaking with love's voice." For times when we want to share deeper, difficult, or sensitive truths, I suggest first asking permission to share. Then we can speak gently, stating *"what's so"* for us without a lot of unnecessary emotion and drama. This means keeping the tone of our voice even and our hearts open. We must also pay attention to keep our communication clean of projections and judgments. We can do this is by speaking our personal truth, which means making subjective statements. For example, if someone is doing something we don't like, we might say "It doesn't feel good to me when you do that," rather than "What you're doing is wrong."

Another way to speak with love's voice is to ask each other the right questions. It's good to ask "What do you need?" or "How do you feel about...?" How often we make assumptions about what someone is thinking or feeling! Checking in with people in this way is so useful. It keeps us current and clear with that person and establishes intimacy on a continual basis.

Many students come to me and ask how they can draw more love into their lives. Sometimes they are looking for that special relationship or maybe they feel a need to connect with others more deeply and open up their hearts a little more. I tell them it's best to give what it is we want to receive, so if it's love we want more of, then we must begin by giving more out and being generous with ourselves in terms of our time, money, vulnerability, and intimacy, practicing the skills outlined in this chapter. One of my students began this process by starting to get to know the people in his office better. He invited one of them to lunch every week, and by the end of a couple of months his whole experience of being in the workplace had improved, as there was so much more intimacy and communication in the office.

Looking through love's eyes...

I went to a wedding once where the pastor invited the couple to "always look at each other through love's eyes." What a difference it makes in our perception of other people when we shift our energy into our hearts and see others with compassion in this way! Can we practice seeing others as our brothers/sisters and treat them as we would wish to be treated? This is acting out the old adage, "Do unto others as you would have done unto you." In this way, every interaction we have with another person can be a "holy encounter."

Our personality is like a mask that we wear. We adorn it when we are born and lose it when we die. It's not really us. When we look at people, we can choose to see beyond the personality, behind the mask, and instead see the true essence of the person as a spiritual being, a child of God, always perfect, always beautiful. True intimacy comes from this. "In-to-me-you-see." Try it and see what a difference it makes in relationships.

Loving our world…

By becoming more conscious of ways to love and respect our environment, we bring our daily life into congruence with our spirituality. We can become more mindful of how we tread on the earth, which may prompt us to do things like exchange harmful chemical cleaning agents for more environmentally-friendly household products, or cut down on our personal use of valuable resources, such as paper or electricity. We might decide to bike rather than drive when we run errands, or to car-pool rather than drive alone; to recycle, re-use or repair items that we may otherwise have discarded; to be careful not to drop trash, or to even pick up other people's trash. All these are acts of love for the earth we live in.

Love appreciates; and taking time to slow down and appreciate the beauty of nature helps us reconnect at a deeper level with ourselves, encouraging us to open our hearts to the wonder of Creation. When we exhibit love for our world, somehow the world gives back, and we feel replenished and energized from the process.

Enriching our lives…

Asking love to guide our choices and behaviors can help empower us and make every moment rich with value and meaning. Keeping this intent in our mind can make every day magical.

> *"When the mind is dissolved, the energy that was involved in the mind becomes love. It has to become something—energy cannot be destroyed. …and in the heart there is no distinction between good and bad. The heart knows no distinction; all distinctions belong to the mind."* —Osho

Examples:

I recently led a yoga vacation to Hawaii. On the way to the airport I had a sudden flash of awareness that the participants had been fooled—they thought they were going there to practice yoga and swim with dolphins, but really they were there to share love. I sat them in a circle on our first night together and told them just that. I added that in practical terms, what that would look like was being on time, being responsible for themselves, being courteous and considerate to others in the group, helping in the kitchen, and speaking up for their needs and sharing from their hearts. The group did exactly that and we had an awesome week, sharing our love and experiencing being in a community that really honored every member and all the people with whom we came in contact along the way.

My friend Frankie had just started a new job. She was determined to be successful at it. After three weeks of long hours and continual effort, she felt frustrated and down on herself, as she was having a hard time mastering what was expected of her. She asked herself what love would do. The answer was clear: Leave and find another job!

Janet buys herself fresh flowers every Monday, just to show herself some appreciation!

I was in the copy shop having copies made. There was a new girl serving at the copy center who was obviously having a hard time keeping up to speed with customer demands. The lady in front of me was definitely irritated with her! When it came to my turn, I was already feeling impatient, and sure enough, the girl messed up my order so I had to wait even longer! I remembered to ask what love would do. The answer was clear: Say something nice and encouraging to this girl who is new and just learning the job. So I thanked her for all her help and gave her a big smile. She seemed surprised but so grateful that I chose to do that rather than give her a hard time! I noticed I felt better too, and my frustration just melted.

Exercises:

Immediate action:

How can you improve the day for anyone you have contact with? Can you offer a compliment to the checkout girl at the supermarket? Call someone special to you and tell them how much you appreciate them? Offer a word of kindness to the waitperson serving your lunch.

Ongoing awareness:

When in any doubt as to what to do or say, ask the question, "What would love do now?" The answer will be very clear.

As part of this exercise, listen with love's ear, speak with love's voice, and see through love's eyes.

There was once a devout man who came to see Ramanuja, the mystic. The man said to Ramanuja, "Show me the way towards the Divine. How can I attain God?"

Ramanuja said, "First, let me ask you a question. Have you ever loved anybody?"

The devotee looked surprised. He said, "What are you talking about? I am a celibate. I don't even look at women—I just close my eyes."

Ramanuja said, "Still, think a little. Has there ever in the past been even a small flickering of love in your heart, for anyone?"

The man said, "But I have come here to learn prayer, not to learn love. Teach me how to pray. And you are talking about worldly things."

Ramanuja became very sad. He said," Then I cannot help you. If you have no experience of love, then there is no possibility for any experience of prayer. So first go into the world and love. And when you have loved and are enriched through it, then come to me. Because only a lover can understand what prayer is."

13
What's necessary?

Conserves our energy

This chapter examines how we spend our energy in the world. Very often our tendency is to speak too much, own too much, and do too much, all of which deplete our energy. Asking "What's necessary?" invites us to take a step back and look clearly to see if we really need to have all the stuff we own, do all the things our minds tell us we "should" do, or say everything that pops into our heads. As we start to simplify, we have more time and energy to spend on things that are really important to us.

How much "stuff" do we really need?

How much do we need to own? How many pairs of shoes do we really need? How large of a house, how well-paid of a job? How many cars and bicycles, holiday homes, and RVs? We live in a material world, and as we get older the tendency is to acquire ever more trappings of wealth in the form of material goods. In my experience, material things take my energy. I feel far freer with less. The greatest feeling of freedom I ever had was in my backpacking days, when all I possessed was a backpack and some clothes as I traveled around the world. In fact, my times of greatest happiness have often been when I've had less in the material sense. I'm older now and have acquired more. But I take heed to buy only what's necessary to enhance my life and not burden myself down with lots of stuff I don't really need.

I notice that friends who have a lot of possessions carry the weight of them in some way. They worry about things being stolen or damaged, they need to attend to insuring everything, or they simply have more things to clean. All this steals our precious energy. I know people with large houses who spend a lot of their free time cleaning instead of spending time on things they really want to be doing. That's fine if cleaning is our passion. But if not, what about hiring a cleaner and giving ourselves time for what really excites us? What's necessary for us to do personally? My business executive friends always say we are better off spending time doing the things we are really good at or that give us the most joy and delegating others to do the rest.

What do we need to do?

Like most of us, I'm a busy person. Occasionally I wake up in the morning and feel overwhelmed when I think about all the things I have to do that day. So I sit down with pen and paper and ask, "What's necessary?" It always turns out that when I really take time to examine my tasks, there are some that need to be done today and others that can be put off until tomorrow. Now my day feels lighter and more manageable. I do the high priority tasks first and the rest get done in a relaxed fashion after that. This sounds so simple a technique, yet it's one of the most useful to practice regularly.

Turning down extra commitments can also be a very healthy thing for us to do, especially if we have a pattern of codependence and people-pleasing behavior. Do we really need to take on that extra task, or would it be more empowering for us to say no?

I have a friend with a large family who all live nearby. He is constantly being asked to do them favors. My friend is a compassionate person and a good listener, and very often they come and visit and dump their problems on him, leaving him feeling drained and tired when they eventually leave. When we worked with "What's necessary?" in our jnana group, he got clear that it was OK to say no to them. He told his father he could not visit and stay all Saturday night just talking. He told his sisters he would not come over and mow their lawns. And what's more, he felt good about this and did not feel guilty! Then he had time for himself and his own life, which brought him far more joy and energy. It also ultimately empowers his family more as they begin to take responsibility for their own lives.

Developing a relationship with uncertainty...

Life presents us with constant challenges and choices. If we are not sure of what to do in any given situation, the answer is...nothing, until the fog in our mind clears—unless, of course, it is necessary to act immediately. If our house is on fire, it is necessary to evacuate the house and call the fire brigade. If our house needs a new coat of paint, but we are not sure if we are going to sell the house or not, asking what's necessary may lead to an answer of "nothing right now," but instead, to wait until the new buyer comes and then they can pick the color of the paint.

Sometimes Time is the great decision maker. We often want to jump to make decisions that may ultimately not serve us. If we are unsure about a course of action, better to wait until other events in our life come along to make the preferred course of action clearer. A useful tool here is to not make decisions in the moment unless absolutely necessary. When someone asks us to do something in the future, we can practice holding off before making a commitment by saying, "I'll get back to you." We can then set up a time to let the person know what we're going to do rather than making a snap decision, allowing time to help us get clearer on what's necessary.

What do we need to say?

How much do we reveal to other people? We all know friends who gossip constantly about others. Is this really necessary, or just idle chitchat? We also all know people who wear their heart on their sleeve and reveal every last detail about themselves to everyone they meet, sucking them into their latest drama. Being aware of what's necessary in our conversations can prevent us from rambling on and on and becoming a bore. It also conserves our energy and encourages us to witness and observe. Talking less can help us to be more present with others, so we can really listen. When we do talk we can choose to share more about our deeper self, our feelings, and our process instead of our stories and gossip.

I had a friend whose mother was always telling her that if only she would cut her hair, wear more make-up, and smile more she would find a man and be much happier. My observation was that this friend was doing just fine the way she was. All the "shoulds" the mother threw at her only served to drive her daughter further away from her, as she really did not want or need her mother's input. Unsolicited advice can feel judgmental and hurtful. It assumes we are not getting life "right."

Sometimes it's hard to hold back our viewpoint when we think we know best. Our desire to fix and change other people can be strong. But instead of volunteering our well-meaning services and opinions, all that is necessary is for us to be available in case someone should ask for assistance. We can certainly invite that availability by letting the person know that we can help them if they so choose. Then if they do, the person will be more able to really receive that help instead of feeling that they are being judged or criticized in any way.

Examples:

I was under a lot of stress one year to cook Thanksgiving dinner for 20 people—including my partner's mother! We had just moved into a new house three weeks previously and didn't have everything "just so." I didn't have matching plates or dining room chairs for that many people. There was a lot I had to do in a short time. I had to ask "What's necessary" and prioritize. I decided to concentrate on the food, and not stress about the un-matched dinner set! The food turned out great and I really don't think anyone cared about the plates (except maybe the mother!). My friends were just happy to all get together for a joyous celebration.

Recently a yoga teacher friend of mine asked me to teach a class for her later that day. I would normally do my best to help her out, but that day when I asked myself what was necessary for me to do, I got a clear inner answer to say no to teaching the class. It was just as well; I felt ill later that day and would not have felt like teaching. I honored myself, and my friend in turn honored my decision.

When I was a sales trainee on my first job, I was sent to a

seminar where they taught us how to sell. One of the main concepts they tried to drum into us was "don't oversell," just do enough to make the sale and no more. Once someone has said they will buy, take the order and go away! So often, inexperienced salespeople will lose the sale by over-selling and talking the buyer out of the deal.

During one of my retreats, a participant shared that he had been feeling sad that day. He had asked the question "What's necessary?" and looked within to see if he needed to fix the feeling and make himself happy somehow. His inner guidance told him to just stay with the sadness and feel it fully until it passed. He did just that.

My friend Linda recently hired two homeless people to help her with a yard project. Over the week she employed them, she observed that they were dirty, underfed, and poorly clothed, and her well-meaning heart wanted to help them. So one day she bundled the two men into her car and took them to the local thrift store so they could buy some clothes. They got there, wandered around, and didn't buy anything. Then she realized she hadn't asked them if they really wanted any new clothes! She had assumed they did because their clothes were so old and dirty. She realized that they had chosen to live the way they did, they were walking their own perfect path, and there was nothing broken about them that needed fixing. In that place, nothing was necessary. She no longer needed to volunteer her services for them, but made it clear that she was available if they ever needed anything.

Exercises:

Immediate action:

For one day (or week), watch your conversation and see how much of what you say is really necessary. Notice if becoming more concise helps you to be more present with others.

Ongoing awareness:

Use "What's necessary?" to help you gain clarity on how to

act or what to do in a given situation, particularly when you are feeling pressured or stressed.

BUTTERFLY'S WINGS

One day as a small opening appeared on a cocoon, a man sat and watched for the butterfly for several hours as it struggled to force its body through that tiny little hole. Then it seemed to stop making any progress. It appeared as if it had gotten as far as it could and it could go no further. So the man decided to help the butterfly. He took a pair of scissors and snipped off the remaining bit of the cocoon. The butterfly then emerged easily. But it had a swollen body and shriveled wings. The man continued to watch the butterfly because he expected that at any moment, the wings would enlarge and expand to be able to support the body, which would contract in time.

Neither happened. In fact the butterfly spent the rest of its life crawling around with a swollen body and shriveled wings. It never was able to fly.

What the man in his kindness and haste didn't understand was that the restricting cocoon and the struggle required for the butterfly to get through the tiny opening were necessary. They were God's way of forcing fluid from the body of the butterfly into its wings so that it would be ready for flight once it achieved its freedom from the cocoon.

Sometimes struggles are exactly what we need in our life. If God allowed us to go through life without any obstacles, it would cripple us. We would not be as strong as we could have been. God gives us difficulties to make us strong, and problems for us to solve. The greater the obstacle, the greater the achievement.

14
What's the hurry?

Teaches patience, reduces stress

I used to be in a hurry to do life. The classic over-achiever, I had goals to meet and deadlines to adhere to. I ran everywhere. I was a great employee, in a hurry to be successful! But after a while, I realized this pressure was self-imposed. I had the rest of my life to make money, have a career, have babies, or build a house. So I left my job and decided to travel around the world.

Life took on a whole different rhythm as I relaxed into the flow of independent and unhurried travel. I realized that many of the things I was in a hurry to achieve were not really important to me at all. I began to cultivate patience, and accept whatever hand life dealt me. I learned to let go of my goal orientation and along with it, my desire to control my life. As I did this, I was able to observe many wondrous events pop up for me, gifts beyond my wildest imaginings, which were much more fulfilling than if I had orchestrated my own agenda.

Attachment to timelines...

There are two kinds of hurrying to look at here. As mentioned above, one is the mind's propensity to want things done by a certain time, which kicks in our desire to manipulate to make this happen. We can call this "attachment to a timeline." Many of us impose timelines upon ourselves that create their own stress and frustration if not fulfilled. Even with this book I have had to resist the temptation to try to get it completed by a certain deadline, when there was no reason to have one.

Artificial goals keep us hooked into the promise of a better future. While goals and dreams are useful for achieving material success in this world, we need to find a balance between being in a hurry to achieve these goals and having the patience to let them unfold gently in their own time. Better to let go of attachment to specific deadlines and be patient instead, trusting that all will happen in perfect timing anyway.

The price of hurry...

The second type of hurry is day-to-day "rushing around." Rushing around clouds our thinking and creates anxiety and stress, which in turn makes us hurry, and the vicious cycle continues. I once asked a doctor friend of mine what he considered to be the leading cause of stress. He said it was the perception that there was not enough time to do all the things that we needed to get done. This stress causes us to dash around attempting to multi-task and get lots of things done at once, but all too often we end up spinning our wheels and becoming less productive from our frantic activity rather than more efficient.

So often this stress is self-imposed. Being in a hurry creates anxiety for us as our mind tells us that we might fail in some way, perhaps by not achieving a certain goal, or by not living up to a particular time agreement. This is not always true or necessary.

When we let go of the hurry, we take the pressure off ourselves and move instead to a place of accepting the situation as it is and trusting that all is in Divine order. For example, if we're late for an appointment and there is nothing we can do about it, can we have faith that all is well anyway? We can choose to arrive at our final destination without melodrama and excuses, without needing to make our late entry special, and instead, just quietly admit that yes, we are running late.

When I hurry, I seem to sabotage myself. I was once in a big hurry to get somewhere and managed to fall and scrape my hand really badly. If I hurry to leave the house I often forget something and have to go back. This has happened so often to me that now I practice activating my witness and watch this tendency of mine to rush. I force myself to slow down, take a breath, and check in with myself before I dash out of the house to see if there is something I still need to do. This way I get to calm any frantic energy and even give my unconscious mind a chance to nudge me in the direction of what I may have forgotten!

More planning...

When we hurry we give ourselves away. What is it that we miss when we don't slow down enough to smell the roses? If we move too fast we can't appreciate the richness of life around us. The sacredness of the moment gets lost as our awareness is focused more on future time rather than on being present here in the Now.

Time agreements do, however, need to be honored as far as possible in order for us to feel good about ourselves and be in integrity. We need to use foresight and plan our day appropriately, which offers yet another opportunity to raise our consciousness. We can choose to make fewer commitments in order to create more time for ourselves to slow down. Learning to say "no" to others when appropriate is a great way for us to honor ourselves, practice our boundaries, and free up our time.

The chemical factor...

We can use our witness consciousness to examine how our daily behaviors and habits set us up for hurry. Many of us rush around because our nervous systems are wired. We drink sodas and espressos and eat sugary desserts, all of which stimulate our systems, creating an adrenaline-style rush that gives us a false and temporary lift of energy to help get us through the day. Then we wonder why we can't sleep at night.

An alternative would be to stay away from caffeine and sugar, drinking more water and herbal teas instead, or eating fruit as a snack or dessert. Once our nervous systems are back in balance we can more easily be calm and centered during our day, and less prone to hurrying.

The value of stillness...

When we take time to practice slowing down we become still

and centered, and more able to draw our energy into ourselves. In this state we embody more fully the essence of our Self, which is what I term as "presence." The more presence we have, the more we magnetically attract what we need into our lives, effortlessly and easily.

One good example of how this works is the story of how I found a publisher for this book. After three years of writing the manuscript I decided it was time to try to find myself an agent to represent me. I had prepared a tip-top marketing plan and proceeded to put a lot of energy into locating the right agent. In the midst of all this activity, I was in a hurry one day and fell on something in my garage, spraining my ankle. Ouch! I couldn't walk for days, and spent a week hobbling around on crutches. I had no choice but to slow down. I meditated more and spent more time in contemplation of my garden. It was as though I was letting myself catch up with myself.

During this time I had a phone conversation with a dear friend who lives in Mount Shasta. She happened to mention a publisher she had just met and suggested that he might be interested in seeing my manuscript. I called him the next day and sent him the marketing plan. Everything flowed very smoothly from that point on, and before I knew it we had a contract. The whole process felt effortless and I strongly believe that the week I had of slowing down allowed the right person to find me rather than me chasing my tail barking up the wrong trees.

Slowing down...

The older I get, the more I experience the value in slowing down. The ideas that "less is more" and "work smart, not hard." I understand that being in a hurry is yet another form of resistance to *what's so.* Nowadays I prefer to surrender to what is happening, with faith and trust that all is in Divine order and the timing is always perfect. As a result I no longer feel stressed, and everything seems to get done with more efficiency, not less. I have let go of my attachments to timelines, and trust that my life will unfold perfectly.

Life is a journey, not a destination.

Examples:

One of my yoga teachers said it took him five years of dedicated practice before he could sit in lotus position! He learned patience and self-acceptance in the meantime, as his body opened gently to the pose.

My friend Lynn-Marie told me of how she used to hate the Christmas holidays. So many presents to buy, so much to do, and so little time to do it all in! It created a big stress for her. One December day she was rushing around shopping for gifts. Suddenly she felt herself get breathless. An anxiety attack was coming on! As she is a nurse, she knew what to do. She stopped what she was doing and sat down, starting to breathe deeply until it passed. Right then and there she decided that this stress was not worth it! She made a decision to get her family gift certificates instead of personally chosen gifts, and promptly took herself home to a nice hot bath and a restful, unhurried evening. She told me she has never allowed herself to get that worked up about Christmas and all the trappings since then and has also not had any more anxiety attacks.

One day one of my students came in late to my hatha yoga class looking breathless and stressed. I noticed that she took a while to settle down into the rhythm and energy of the practice. After class we talked about what was going on for her and she got to see the absurdity of how she had been anxiously hurrying to yoga class, where she was going to unwind and let go of her stress! I suggested that instead she would have been better served to have accepted the fact that she was going to be late. She could then slow down and be calm before entering the class environment rather than having to "hurry up and relax!"

Exercises:

Immediate action:

Be aware this week of when you are in a hurry and what that does to your nervous system. Can you at this moment stop and look to do it differently, to take the pressure off yourself?

Ongoing awareness:

Look at the bigger picture of your life and your attachments to goals with timelines. Try letting go of these attachments, giving yourself the opportunity to practice patience and surrender instead.

There once were two monks sitting under a tree meditating on their enlightenment. One day a pilgrim passed by. "Where are you going?" asked one of the monks.

"To see God," the pilgrim replied.

"Well, when you see him can you please ask how long I'm going to have to sit here and meditate before I get my enlightenment?" the elder monk asked.

"I will," replied the pilgrim, and he was gone.

Weeks later the pilgrim returned. "Did you see God?" the elder monk asked.

"Yes," replied the pilgrim.

"So what did he say?" the monk questioned eagerly.

The pilgrim replied, "God said that you had only three more lifetimes to go before you obtain enlightenment."

"Whoopee!" exclaimed the monk! "Only three lifetimes to go!"

The pilgrim then turned his attention to the younger monk. "Aren't you curious about what God has in store for you?"

"I'm only a novice," said the monk, "but if it pleases you I will hear the truth of it."

The pilgrim pointed to the tree above them, in full bloom with a proliferation of leaves. "God says that as many leaves as are on that tree, that is the number of lifetimes you will have to live before you receive your enlightenment."

"Whoopee!" said the younger monk, and jumped up and down with joy.

The older monk looked at him curiously. "Why are you so happy?" he asked. "Don't you see how many leaves the tree has left on its branches?"

"Yes," replied the younger monk. "But don't you understand? I'm happy because God said I **will** *get my enlightenment!" And with that there was a big gust of wind and all the leaves were blown from the tree.*

BREAKING OLD PATTERNS

Breaking our ingrained patterns is really the juice, the golden nugget of our consciousness work, so many benefits does it yield. In this section we learn to break free of old conditioning so that we no longer need to continue repeating the same mistakes and attracting the same type of occurrences into our lives.

Once we break away from our familiar way of doing things we are free to dive into the unknown and surrender up control of our lives so that Divine Will can truly enter in and guide us willingly to our destiny.

15
What's the lesson?

Helps us to not repeat the same old behaviors

Do you ever wonder why rotten things happen to great people? Why life just doesn't seem fair sometimes, particularly when awful things are going on in our lives and we just can't fathom what we may have done to deserve such calamities?

In every situation we can choose to play the victim or take responsibility for the situation and find the silver lining in the cloud. Life presents us with challenges and tests for our greater good. How could there be a victory if there was no struggle? Struggles are there for us to learn from. Wouldn't life be bland without them? The wonderful thing about life is that if we don't get the message the first time around, we will no doubt be presented with the opportunity to have another shot at it at a later date with new players in a new drama. Life themes have a tendency to recur until we get the lesson.

The question here is, how much can we pay attention so as to grow and evolve from life's obstacles and not have to repeat the same errors again and again? Asking "What's the lesson?" gives us an opportunity to activate our loving witness consciousness and look objectively at any situation. If we can see our role in it clearly, then when the same situation occurs again we have a better chance of doing it differently and breaking free of our patterns.

I have a psychic healer friend who has made a career out of paying attention to seemingly insignificant occurrences. He says everything has purpose, nothing is random, and when we train ourselves to pay attention to subtleties we can find an incredible richness in the tapestry that is our life. We get to be able to use the events in our life to enhance our consciousness so that we can get our lessons with the swish of a peacock feather rather than with a sledgehammer over the head. The choice is ours.

When we need more clarity...

When we commit to seeing every situation as an opportunity for growth and learning, we find that even the ugliest occurrences can hold hidden gems of insight. However, if the life challenge is particularly painful or we are very enmeshed and embroiled in our daily lives, it is hard for us to perceive clearly and get these insights. If this is happening and we can't see the wood for the trees, one way out of this is to take a break away from our routines and take some time to go within. I have often found that when I remove myself from a situation and create distance between myself and it, then I can more easily look back and see what my role has been and own my piece of the puzzle.

Setting ourselves up with quiet time to walk or meditate is a great way to go within and connect with the wise part of us we might call the "higher self" or "inner teacher." When we get quiet, we are more able to call on this part of ourselves to help us find the learning. If it doesn't come immediately, pray for it, ask for it, and be open to listening to whatever insights pop into awareness. The answers always lie within each one of us.

Transforming our perspective...

If someone wrongs us, what are we to do? For example, if somebody we have trusted steals from us, what are we to make of it? We can blame them, criticize their actions, and feel sorry for ourselves. Or, we can take responsibility for the event and see that we could have been more discerning in our association with that person. We could have protected ourselves better, heeded subtle warning signs that something was wrong, and certainly we could have listened more to our inner guidance, which was screaming at us to disassociate from this person. If we can learn all these things from this one incident, what a gift it was. Forgiveness can then come easily, as we see that the whole scenario was a set-up for us to get these lessons, so next time we can learn to take better care of ourselves.

So many of life's lessons seem to be there for us to learn to trust our feelings and inner guidance. If we view life this way, then where is there any room for judgment as to whether what is happening is good or bad? It is simply there for our benefit, for us to learn and grow from. In that place, we can be grateful for all of it. This gives us a way to make sense of our world, experiencing the richness it offers as we explore the impact and nuance of every event in our life.

> *"Have faith in Allah, but tie up your camel!"*
> —Old Arabic saying

The body as a guide...

The body is a great barometer for knowing when we are on or off track. For me, my second cervical vertebra goes out of alignment when I am stressed or something is up for me to look at. A relatively subtle body change like that offers us the peacock feather opportunity for learning lessons. But sometimes we need the sledgehammer. A major health scare such as a heart attack is normally a pretty effective wake-up call for us to make lifestyle changes. My father had a heart attack a few years ago, which prompted him to get clear that he needed to retire from work and spend more time with his family and friends. He hasn't regretted that decision at all!

Pain is an honored teacher—after all, it gets our undivided attention. The body was built to be a perfect machine. If it is not functioning at optimal health something is going on in our lives that is causing this. My psychic healer friend can always see the patterns we create in our consciousness that form dis-ease and illness. The good news is that we can also reverse those patterns and regain our health, with the right guidance and commitment to our healing.

As an example, when I met my last partner, I gave up a lot of my yoga teaching and worked full-time with him in his company. After a few months I began to notice I felt tired and sluggish. I eventually went to the doctor and was diagnosed with severe anemia. When I spent some time meditating on why this was happening, I realized that it was because I was off my life path. I was giving my power away to my partner to help him fulfill his dreams at the expense of my own. After this light bulb had gone on in my head, I gradually withdrew from the corporate world and went back to my own work. My health improved and my own career began to blossom.

> *"Life is a teacher to the wise man, and an enemy to the fool."*—Ancient proverb

Co-dependence vs. growth...

Too much caring can take away people's lessons. When we are co-dependent with our loved ones and friends, constantly excusing them and picking them up when they have fallen down, we hurt both them and us. Rescuing others from feeling the depths of their pain serves no-one. Only when we are allowed to plumb these depths will it potentially hurt enough for the lesson to be learned and for growth to occur.

My friend Joanne has an alcoholic drug-addicted son. This son worked for Joanne in her business and lived in her house, although he was over 30 years old. For a while Joanne turned her gaze away from what was happening under her very nose and was in denial about the truth of her son's addictions. However after a while it became too obvious. He stopped eating, showed up for work late, and started to steal from her.

Joanne eventually confronted him and offered to pay for him to go to a rehabilitation center. He refused, denying that there was anything wrong. So Joanne fired him and threw him out of the house, practicing painful but courageous "tough love." She let him go, knowing that if she continued to support his behavior he would never heal. Indeed, her son ended up on the streets for a while. Eventually, however, he hit bottom and sought professional help. He has since joined Alcoholics Anonymous and has been clean and sober for a few months now. He empowered himself to turn his life around and got his lessons. Joanne has been able to resume her relationship with him and there is now a mutual and healthy respect between mother and son.

Ultimately...

Ultimately there is only one lesson to be learned, and that is to experience life fully, learning to be as conscious as we can be with whatever situation comes our way.

> *"Adversity is like a strong wind. It tears away from us all but the things that cannot be torn, so that we see ourselves as we truly are."*
> —Arthur Golden, *Memoirs of a Geisha*

Examples:

One of my friends is very wealthy but used to attract people into his life who would steal from him. He could not understand why, and complained that he couldn't trust anyone and that he was a victim of terrible circumstance. Eventually he asked himself what the lesson was here and began to own that he had some responsibility for this situation too. With the help of a therapist he realized that he was running an internal tape that said he did not deserve to have nice things in life, so on an unconscious level he was creating situations whereby people would take from him. Once he got clarity on this and changed his internal tape, he no longer attracted theft.

I used to attract men into my life who would criticize me and abandon me in some way. After three relationships in a row like this, I began to see the pattern emerging—and the common denominator was me! When I took the time to be still and ask myself what the lesson was here, I saw that I had actually abandoned myself on some level. I had allowed men to walk all over me and surrendered my power to them without standing up for my own needs and wants. Once I realized that, my relationships shifted and I no longer drew men into my life that treated me that way.

A friend's car broke down at my house after a party. She is a nurse and had to leave early for work the next day. Two other friends kindly offered to drive her home and pick her up to take her to work the next day. This made her very uncomfortable. She found it very hard to accept their kindness and it became clear that her resistance to receiving was exactly why this situation occurred—her lesson was to learn to receive graciously! Once she understood that, my nurse friend gratefully accepted the offer of a ride home.

The student asked the Master,
"Why are lessons hard?"
"Because we want valid victories!"
the Master replied. "If the lesson were
too easy it would invalidate the victory!"

Exercises:

Immediate action:

Look at a recurring unpleasant situation in your life. Take a few quiet moments to go within. First, own that you are responsible for your reaction to the situation. Ask what the lesson is. Pay attention to what your intuition tells you here.

Ongoing awareness:

Examine the relationships in your life for signs of co-dependent behavior. Are there people in your world who are somehow preventing you from getting your lessons? Or, are you acting in an overcaring way with someone else, and preventing them from getting theirs? Start to cut out all co-dependent rescuing behavior.

A cynical reporter from a foreign newspaper traveled to Japan to interview a wise man. When he arrived, he was invited in and offered some tea. The wise man began pouring the tea into his cup and continued pouring and pouring until the tea overflowed the cup and ran down onto the table.

"What are you doing?" asked the reporter? "My cup is already full!"

"Yes and your mind is full like this cup," said the wise man. "Come back when you are empty and ready to hear what I have to say."

With that the surprised reporter got up and left. He had been denied his interview but had received a valuable lesson instead.

16

What's the melodrama?

Diffuses our tendency to overreact

There are some people who, when asked how they are, proceed to relate a tale of never-ending woe and suffering, starting with when they ran over the family hamster with their car on the way to see their doctor about some chronic disease that we've never heard of! Whenever their life threatens to run smoothly, another significant event magically happens again, making their life one drama after another and thrusting them once more into the limelight as the center of everyone's attention and pity.

Melodrama is the ego's device for grabbing energy and attention from others. Life is happening to us and "isn't it awful!" The drama king/queen takes no responsibility for life's events. Instead, they invite the mentality of victimhood, the "poor me" syndrome. Deep down, this need for drama is rooted in a sense of unworthiness. The less worthy and the emptier we feel inside, the more our tendency to fill this aching hole with energy-grabbing dramatics.

Nothing is special...

Melodrama is the stuff of soap operas. It creates an emotional roller coaster to thrill and entertain...or bore, depending on our viewpoint! The question is, can we step out of the drama and instead be in our loving witness consciousness where we can observe clearly, rather than getting enmeshed in the soap opera of life? Acting out melodrama takes us into emotional states where we cannot as easily find our lesson or act appropriately from a centered space. When we make an event significant and special and allow ourselves to spin from one emotional extreme to its polar opposite, we experience life as a turbulent ride of ups and downs, neither of which are helpful for our clarity and higher awareness.

Instead, we can choose to find some middle ground where we can be more centered, calm, and observant. There's nothing that hasn't happened in a similar way before and won't happen again. The only constant is change. How we perceive that change is the issue. We can observe it quietly, with gratitude, or we can make a big song and dance about it. It's our choice. All situations can either be dealt with or accepted. In truth, all things will pass in time. When we are 90 years old and looking back on our life from our rocking chair, will the events we are concerned with now really matter? From the perspective of time and hindsight they may just look like perfect transitions. Even when so-called "big" events happen in our lives, such as bankruptcy, divorce, or illness, we can choose to remain centered and stay out of melodrama. Rather, we can focus on sharing our current feelings and finding solutions for ourselves, instead of continuing to relate our sad story to everyone around us.

An example of a person acting with grace in a difficult situation, rather than doing melodrama, is Ram Dass. Ram Dass is an ex-Harvard professor, a spiritual teacher and author of *Be Here Now.* A few years ago he suffered a stroke that nearly killed him. One side of his body was mostly paralyzed. He used to be a great speaker. Now his speech is slurred and he has trouble finishing sentences. He could have felt very victimized from this stroke. Instead, he has chosen to see it as an opportunity for more spiritual growth, authoring a book which talks about the challenges of aging, *Still Here: Embracing Aging, Changing, and Dying,* and continuing his numerous lecturing engagements despite his difficulties with speech. Although physically challenged, he has remained centered and grounded in his spiritual practices, accepting his new situation with equanimity and joy.

Melodrama vs. passion...

We can distinguish melodrama from passion. Passion is our

ability to feel deeply. It is not based in ego, but comes from the higher Self. It has the energy to move us through life in a purposeful way, propelling us to act out our heart's delight in ways that nurture and delight the soul. Examples of this are the many famous singers, artists, and writers who let this creative energy move through them, expressing themselves with their art as a result.

Situation comedies...

Being aware of our own tendency to go into melodrama is the first step towards making a change in our behavior. We can catch ourselves in the moment as we launch into our dramatic story, and cut it off right there. Then we can be empowered to make different choices in how we respond to situations. We can even start turning our melodramas into situation comedies by not taking ourselves so seriously and seeing the lighter side of life. After all, we humans are such curiously odd creatures. We do such funny things!

I was traveling in Bali with two friends and we had hired a driver to take us on a four hour trip across the island. My friend Eric started to get annoyed when the driver drove fast over the bumpy road and he banged his head on the ceiling of the car. He yelled at the driver, asking him to slow down, but to no avail. The more annoyed he got, the bumpier the road became, and the less the driver could have cared! Eric began to get even more frustrated. He started to criticize the driver for not repairing his shocks! And for not having more respect for his car, and us...but nothing changed the driving style of our chauffeur!

Meanwhile, my other friend, Rick, and I were trying hard to control our laughter, so ludicrous did the situation look to us, until we could contain ourselves no longer. We both burst out laughing at the big fuss Eric was making! There was nothing much we could do about the state of the car, just accept the bumpiness and deal with it! Luckily, Eric began to see the funny side too and we all laughed hysterically the rest of the journey whenever the driver hit a bump!

Other people's dramas...

Drama kings and queens use their problems to define

themselves. They identify with suffering and misery, which gives them a false sense of self, based on a deep core feeling of unworthiness. The ego, in a desperate attempt to feel worthy and grab attention from others, perpetuates this false identification with suffering, especially if the person finds support for their position of victim from others around them.

Most of us have friends who are constantly doing this song and dance. These people want to pull us into their personal dramas, getting us to engage emotionally with them as support players in their cast. We don't need to go there. If we do, it can be emotionally and energetically very draining.

When people try to engage us in this way, we have some choices in how to respond. Firstly, we can listen to them without giving their story any feedback or energy. If we just listen without engaging, often the story will just fizzle out. Sometimes people just need to be heard. They are not looking for a solution. They just want to feel that they are right and that someone is on their side. If they can feel acknowledged, their need for melodrama often dissolves.

My friend Rick runs a small hotel, and his employees love to come to him with their workplace dramas. Once they launch into their story, he will stop them and ask if they are looking for a solution or if they just want to vent. If they just want him to hear them out, he will listen and then send them on their way. If they are seeking solutions, he will help with that. He does not hook into their dramas! If he did, he would be exhausted at the end of each day!

Another strategy is to ask the person what is really underlying their drama. Quite often the tendency to emotional dramatics is only a symptom for deeper personal issues. Once those issues are uncovered and acknowledged, the need for dramatics is often gone. We can then help our friends with processing their emotions, staying in present time with what is happening for them right now.

Sometimes people's need for melodrama is so great that they are not prepared to look for solutions or move beyond the chaos and emotional turbulence. In this circumstance we have a right to tell that person that we no longer wish to hear their story! We have a responsibility to ourselves for our own energy, and supporting their victim consciousness serves no-one. It is just a bottomless pit of neediness that sucks other people dry.

While it is wholly appropriate for us to feel our emotions fully in the moment, holding on to the emotion in the form of a dramatic story after the event has passed perpetuates the chaos. We can really serve our friends by calmly guiding them to either a place of acceptance of what has occurred if there is nothing to be done about it, or we can encourage them to take appropriate action to move forward. End of story!

Internalizing our melodramas...

Some of us hold our melodramas inside our heads in the form of anxiety and self-pity. We re-run the movie of some past event and its effect on us until, like a deeply-etched groove in a broken record, the emotion surrounding the event remains with us. Indeed, as we continue to identify as victims in our heads, the world will reflect that consciousness and continue to supply us with ways to feel victimized! Form follows consciousness. This is why "bad" things sometimes happen to "nice" people (victims). This identification with pain can actually feel comforting for some people, who are used to using it to gain sympathy and attention. This can be a tough habit to break, but break it we must to free ourselves from the pull of a toxic past that colors our experience of now.

To do this we must again enlist the help of our witness. We can watch when we tell our sad story of victimization, either in our head or out loud, and make conscious efforts to stop it. Instead, as we learn to identify more with our witness and less with our past and our personality, a new way of relating can be discovered, based on present time, which yields a greater depth of intimacy and is ultimately much more fulfilling.

The melodrama of gossip...

My friend Adair calls gossip "a cheap way to relate." When we gossip, we talk about people behind their backs, usually in a judgmental, melodramatic way, rather than enjoying a more intimate, personal conversation with the person we are with. As teenagers we tend to gossip as a way to boost our own sense of self-worth at the expense of other people. As we get older and mature and become more aware of the negative impact of gossip, both for ourselves and for the person being discussed, we begin to refrain from this habit. Except that some of us don't!

Friends of mine who work in offices come to jnana yoga and talk about their challenge of not being sucked into the office gossip pool. They observe that many of their colleagues are bored at work and gossip in order to spice up their lives and feel self-righteous! The more dramatic the gossip, the more attention is commanded. Hence the tendency to blow things up out of all proportion, beyond what is real, for the purpose of entertainment. My jnana yoga students gently steer their colleagues away from gossiping about other people and towards more intimate connection by asking them more about themselves. In this way office relations improve and there is a more positive atmosphere in the workplace.

The role of the media....

The media has a vested interest in our attention. It feeds upon our collective need for melodrama. That is why the news media, especially, loves big, dramatic news stories to draw in the audience and keep us tuned in. It is important to become aware of the effects of media reporting on our consciousness. Reported news is generally bad news given as dramatic a spin as possible. Do we really need to spend an hour a day or more listening to bad news? What does this do to us? One way to find out is to practice a media fast for a month or so and see how our lives change when we no longer tune in to the mass media. Another way is to observe the media from the point of view of the dispassionate witness, noticing any tendency to become emotionally hooked into any of the stories. This is harder, as we are often unaware of the subtle effects of negative news reporting on our psyche.

The media's power to create fear and chaos amongst the general population became abundantly clear after the 9/11 terrorist attack. As conscious beings, we can choose not to hook into mass negative consciousness. Indeed, it is important that we not do so, that we choose instead to anchor the vibration of love and compassion rather than fear and hatred. If we have to turn our televisions off in order to do that, then so be it!

All the world's a stage...

Shakespeare remarked that "all the world's a stage." Indeed, on some level, we're all playing our roles to perfection with God as the director. We've chosen the parts we are playing today, but we all may play all of the roles at some time or another. Knowing this helps us to let go of judgments, victimhood, and over-dramatization. We can take a step back with the help of our witness and observe life's events with curiosity and calmness, as though we are in the audience rather than on the stage.

The fool laughs at others.
The wise man laughs at the world.
The sage laughs at himself.

Examples:

When I was married, my husband and I lived in a house that had particularly beautiful long gray curtains in the dining room. We also had a gray cat called "Blue." Blue had been neutered, or so we thought. One day we were sitting having dinner and I saw Blue walk into the room, casually lift up his hind leg, and spray our beautiful curtains in a perfect arch of yellow cat liquid! On closer examination it was clear that the cat still had his private parts. I was furious and made a huge melodrama out of this, bewailing the fact that my curtains were ruined forever. When the day came that we lost the house to foreclosure, I remember thinking about how worthless all that anger and upset had been. It just didn't matter anymore and my melodrama at the time certainly hadn't changed anything.

My friend Ray got a letter from the IRS. He panicked. "Oh my God—I'm being audited by the IRS! How terrible! Where are my tax papers? Who can help me? What if I owe them money!" He made a big fuss to all his friends and was so scared he did not dare to open the letter for a week. When he finally did, he found a check enclosed—they owed him a refund! The melodrama was for nothing.

My friend Mike took his car to the carwash, handed over the keys, and settled down to read the newspaper. Twenty minutes later he looked up to see someone driving off with his newly cleaned car! Mike studies jnana yoga with our group and was quickly able to switch on his witness consciousness and observe calmly the theft of his car without drama. Indeed, his car was eventually recovered. He got a really good settlement from the insurance company and bought himself a nice new car that he is ultimately much happier with. All this was achieved by going through the motions of reporting the theft and making the insurance claim. Mike chose not to make himself the victim of the theft. He had no need to relate his sad story to people. Instead he just dealt with his situation as required and got it handled without any unnecessary gnashing of teeth!

My friend Tom is an adult child of an alcoholic. He says that as a child he would never know if he was coming home to a happy, normal household or to a house where Mom and Dad were screaming at each other and where there was complete chaos. This constant household drama was the pattern of life he knew. As a result, he has continued to create drama in his adult life to unconsciously play out the familiar patterns of childhood. He is always running late and only just catching planes, "accidents" happen to him all the time, and he always lives on the edge financially, wondering every month if there will be enough money for rent. He is now aware of this pattern and is consciously trying to let go of the need for recreating drama, replacing it with healthier behavior.

Exercises:

Immediate action:

Think about the last few times you did melodrama, when you got really upset about something and screamed, shouted, or became obsessed. Look back now and see whether getting so emotional did anything to help the situation. Did it matter anyway?

Ongoing awareness:

Hold the thought that nothing is special and change is the only constant. Use this to help you stop reacting to situations and instead become the observer. Can you take the e-motion out of the situation? Emotion is energy in motion.

Three wise men went to visit the King. The King wanted them to prove their wisdom. He said he would give them anything in the Kingdom if they could give him something that would make him sad when he was happy and happy when he was sad.

They returned and gave the King a piece of paper. He said, "Give them whatever they desire!"

The paper said, "All things will pass."

17

How do I know?

Frees us from limiting belief systems

I was an intellectual as a child and taught myself to read at the age of three. My nose was always stuck in a book and when I went to school at age five, I was already well-versed in children's literature. Being inclined towards academics, I naturally became a good and enthusiastic student and went on to university to get my degree in Business Studies with German.

Being in my head was a safe and comfortable place for me. It was my arena of competence and security, where I knew I could shine and outperform others. The only trouble was, I was so well trained in the academic arena that this attitude of "I know" spilled over into my everyday life and colored my existence. I was so sure I was right that I often would not be open to exploring other possibilities. And of course, I was very often not right.

I have since learned the price I paid for being in my known. "I know" says "I will not learn." It keeps us stuck, fixed in our position, rigid and limited in our current reality without inviting in the possibility to look at other options. This is because all absolutes like *never, always, can't,* and *I'm sure* are based on the small amount of knowledge and experience that we have gleaned from our life to date.

Our known world is comfortable and familiar, and it is therefore hard for us to break our patterns around it. However, there is always going to be an infinite bank of knowledge and possibility out there that we have yet to discover which would potentially change our perspective.

Who's right?

"I know" breeds the attitude of "I'm right." When we are around people who know they are always right, we can probably attest to the fact that there is no room for anyone else in a relationship with them. It gets hard to be around them and it's quite a barrier to intimacy. Many people who are always "right" get to be alone a lot. My friend Jayne always tells me that when she was single she got to be right about everything!

> *"Opinions are man's main limitations."* —Barry Long

What's the assumption?

The other aspect of knowing that we encounter is assumptions. When we assume we know what someone wants without first asking, we take away that person's choice. For example, my grandmother would always assume that I wanted dessert and would give it to me without checking with me first. I would feel obliged to eat it whether I wanted it or not. If we are not sure, it's better to ask the person and get clarity rather than assuming we know what's right for them. We have to resist the temptation to project our ideas, needs, and wants on others around us.

Inviting the clarity...

The opposite of "I know" is "I don't know," that is, playing in our unknown, where we are more open to experiencing whatever arises without prejudice. There are now an infinite number of possibilities for us. We are no longer limited. In this place, clarity can show up. At first it might be just a little bit of clarity, and then with time and patience we can open up a space in our life for more and more clarity to appear, so we can get clearer and clearer about the courses of action available to us.

I am reminded here of a Bruce Lee movie where our hero is trapped in a seemingly impossible situation with no way out. In the realm of his known, certain death awaits. However, instead of panicking, he calmly sits down on the floor and meditates until the solution for escape presents itself! He allows the solution to arise from within his unconscious rather than relying on his limited mind to provide the answer!

> *"Believe in nothing—let everything be sacred."*
> —Yogi Baba

Letting go of belief...

As we explore our unknown more and more, we eventually hit up against our belief systems. We might call this "thinking in the box." For example, I may think I know that eating chocolate is bad for me and that if I drink two margaritas I always get a headache. I tell myself that my body can't bench press 200 pounds and my brain is not capable of learning Chinese. If we continue to think in this way we will undoubtedly stay stuck in the same reality. But what if we are wrong? What if we are selling ourselves a fiction? People used to believe the world was flat and if we kept on sailing west we would fall right off the earth. No-one thought it was possible to run a four-minute mile until Roger Bannister proved otherwise. Once that belief was changed, lots of people began to run that fast. So we see that as we begin to drop our belief systems and our conversational use of absolutes, more and more miracles can enter our life and what is possible can start to show up.

Challenging situations can make us feel like we can't cope or do not have resources to deal with our situation. But what if this is not true? We all have unlimited resources within. The ego keeps this in check so we stay in our limited perspective of "I can't" and "I don't know how," which prejudge our lack of ability. What if we do know how and we can? As with the Bruce Lee example, maybe resources can show up from unconsidered sources.

"I don't know" invites us to pause and face our emptiness. It's only apparently empty. If we can get past the fear of remaining empty and powerless and start from a place of innocence, we can begin to take baby steps out of it, forming intentions of what is needed and focusing on desired outcome without having to know the means with which we will achieve it. We can simply ask that the universe support us in this intention over time. Rather than needing to see the entire big picture solution, we can ask to see the next step. We can be present with that, then ask for the next one, and so on, remaining in our center and our unknown as the mystery continues to unfold.

Intuitive knowing...

Knowing in our heads is different from the inner knowing of our hearts, that place of intuition. We need to learn to differentiate between that gut feeling "knowingness" that guides us from within, and the voice in our heads that tells us something based on past experience. With intuitive knowing we often have a visceral feeling in our body about what is right. We have no need to argue with anyone about it. We just know. By contrast, with head knowing we often feel a need to validate ourselves and argue our point!

My friend Jill was exploring the dating scene and got a call from someone with a foreign accent who had seen her ad in the personals and wanted to go out with her. Her mind told her that this person is from a different culture and may therefore be very incompatible with her, but somehow her inner knowing overruled that idea. She checked in with her gut feeling which told her to go ahead and make the date. "There's something there for me," she thought. "This just feels right." She met the person and discovered that he was absolutely delightful. They had a wonderful time together and entered into a long-term relationship.

> *" In the beginners' mind there are many possibilities, but in the expert's there are few."*
> —Shunryu Suzuki, *Zen Mind, Beginner's Mind*

Knowing vs. faith...

If there's no uncertainty in our life, there is no room for trust and faith. What if we could lead our lives with so much faith that we expected miracles to occur? Surrendering the need to know "how," we can pray for a desired outcome, offer it to God, let it go, and see what happens. Then allow ourselves to be delightfully surprised!

> *The Queen said to Alice, who was standing in a world she did not believe, "I dare say, you have not had much practice. Why, sometimes I have believed as many as six impossible things before breakfast."*
> —Lewis Carroll, *Alice Through the Looking Glass*

Examples:

I first came over to the U.S. at the age of 21 and hitch-hiked around the country for 10 weeks with a friend. I loved our trip but when I returned to England and was asked how it was, I said, "Great, but I'd never want to live there." Fortunately, I did not stick to this particular absolute! Ten years later I married an American and we moved to California. I've been here ever since and I love it!

My mother always used to say she hates foreign food. She wouldn't even try it. It was good, plain British fare or nothing! She "knew" she wouldn't like anything else! This changed when she came to visit me in the States. We went to visit a friend of mine who is Korean. My friend had cooked an incredible feast of Korean delicacies for us! My mom had no choice but to eat it—and guess what? She loved it! Now she is less resistant to new foods and new experiences!

I used to be a vegetarian and swore I would never eat red meat again as long as I lived! But after a severe bout of anemia I now have a high protein, low carbohydrate diet that serves me very well and I do occasionally eat lamb!

I work with a psychic healer friend teaching seminars on developing intuition. The first time we set about planning our seminar, we worked out a format and I said, "Great. I will write this down and this can be what we will present." I had a definite "need" to know what we were going to do. He, on the other hand, was not of the same opinion! "This could all change by tomorrow—a better way may show up," was his thought. It turned out he was right! On the day a whole new piece of information came into our consciousness that felt more appropriate for us to share! It was a great lesson to me to let go of my need to know.

A few years ago I attended a fire-walking seminar. We spent the first couple of hours raising our energy with team-building exercises and getting more and more excited about challenging our fears. Then came the moment of truth—the coals were ready! In order to walk across we had to ignore our minds, which said, "Don't be crazy—you'll burn yourself if you do that!" Instead, we watched our instructor go across the coals and in a frenzy of "can-do-ness" followed him into the fire. We all did it just fine—without any burns at all!

> *The unknown—*
> *a stepping off point for the mind to let go.*
> *The unknowable—questions that have no answers.*
> *The inconceivable—the question disappears.*

Exercises:

Immediate action:

For one day, cut out the words *I'm sure, I know, never,* and *always* from your speech. Replace them with words that invite more possibility, such as *maybe, possibly, perhaps,* or *as of yet.*

Ongoing awareness:

Can you build a relationship with uncertainty and stay in your "I don't know?" Cultivate an attitude of listening instead of having strong opinions.

There once was an old lady who was at the airport waiting for a plane. She had a box of cookies with her. She started reading the paper to pass the time. Presently a man came and sat down next to her. There was a little table between them and the box of cookies was on that table. The lady looked out of the corner of her eye with some amazement as the man reached over and took one of the cookies.

"Well," she thought, "He must be hungry. I won't say anything." She took another cookie. And then he took another. And so on, until there was just one cookie left. At this point the man took the last cookie, broke it in two, and offered her half. She accepted, while thinking, "Of all the nerve!"

A few minutes later they boarded the plane. As she loaded her carry-on bag into the overhead rack, her unopened box of cookies fell out. She had absent-mindedly been eating his cookies the whole time!

18

Who's in control?

Allows the flow of life to enter in

Control is futile. Those with a need to control are fighting a losing battle. For starters, there are six billion people on the planet who need to be controlled. Then there's the weather, appliances that break down, the car, machinery, the dog that chews your sock, and the cat that pees on your new shag rug. If we need to be in control, there will always be something for us to get upset about, forever.

Control is about using our will to affect an outcome. It's a belief system that says that if we let go of the control, bad things will happen to us. It's based in fear. We hold on tightly to life, contracting our body, getting upset. We are under the illusion that control will make us safe, but in actuality, the opposite is true. We are more vulnerable when we try to control outcomes, as we are resisting what wants to happen. Imagine being on the chiropractor's table ready for an adjustment. When we tense up, it hurts and the adjustment is not as effective. When we relax and surrender, the doctor is able to adjust our bones more easily and safely.

We need to differentiate between appropriate and inappropriate control. Control is useful in many circumstances. Disciplining children to give them a sense of healthy boundaries, containing our anger in a business meeting, or using our will to be disciplined in practicing a challenging activity when our tendency is to be lazy are all examples of appropriate use of control. It's the overuse of our willpower to make things happen the way we think they should that gets us into trouble and takes so much of our energy. Anything created from the will of the ego can never produce an enduring sense of satisfaction and contentment because when we use our will we are obstructing the flow of life. It is our resistance to life's flow that makes us upset and uncomfortable.

Self-control...

Where I grew up in England we were always taught to be in control of our feelings. Crying in public was frowned upon. Anger was tightly reigned in and everybody was "nice." There was no honesty. You never really knew how anyone felt about anything. In uncomfortable situations everyone was encouraged to "soldier on" (which means grin and bear it). That military attitude pervades our private school system in Britain even today and eventually trickles down through society to become the norm. Letting go of that conditioning and learning to surrender to life's flow has been one of my hardest challenges.

Society teaches us to control our image. From a young age we observe others around us conforming to "normal" rules of behavior. In an effort to be accepted and loved, we too begin to don the mask of personality and of controlled responses. We start to lose touch with our sense of authentic Self and with our deeper soul urges as this personality gradually takes over our functioning. An important part of jnana yoga is the process of using our witness consciousness to help us unravel this mask to discover what is lying hidden beneath it—our true, authentic, spontaneous Self, magnificent in its Presence.

When others control us...

Sometimes we give our power away to others and allow another person to control us. This keeps us weak, so we remain under the illusion that we need the other person. We may do this to gain approval or to please our controller, because on some level we don't feel worthy. This dynamic sets up an energy leak from the third chakra, the energy center that governs our self-esteem and causes us to start to lose our sense of self.

We can observe the children of controlling parents to be deferential, disempowered, and frightened, as though the spirit of the child has retreated elsewhere. With the prevalence of control in our society is it any wonder that we have produced a nation of fearful adults? Similarly, we all know browbeaten women who are completely dominated by their husbands. They no longer have an opinion about anything. They defer to their husband for all decisions and have completely lost themselves in the relationship. This kind of violation does not feel good and needs to end, either by healing the factors that led to this control/domination dynamic or by leaving the relationship. These persons need to find within themselves their own sense of empowerment in order to get free from the grip of the tyrant.

Controlling others...

When we control others, not only does it take a lot of our own energy to do so. but we also prevent people from learning their lessons and making their own mistakes. This can do tremendous damage to our psyche, even if well-intentioned, particularly if this controlling behavior is directed at us as children.

All the time I lived at home my mother never allowed me to do anything in the kitchen. She thought I would make a mess, and besides she could handle the cooking more efficiently than I. As a result I have struggled with my relationship with the kitchen. I have an internal tape that says, "I can't cook, I'm messy, and I'm not to be trusted with food." Indeed I have borne this out to be true very often by burning either myself or the food on many occasions. If my mom had let me help her with cooking, the very worst that could have happened was that I may have made a mess! At least I would have had a chance to learn from my mistakes and gain some of my mother's culinary knowledge!

My friend Judy's mother never trusted her to have her own money as a child. Her mother was afraid that Judy would make poor choices and squander her pocket money, so she simply did not give her any. The opportunity for Judy to make her own choices with money was not there. Gone, too, was the chance for her to learn the value of money and how to budget and save. From this controlling action on behalf of her mother, Judy laid down an internal tape that she was not to be trusted with money and that money was scarce. As a result she has had poverty issues all her life that she is only now beginning to unravel.

Controlling our world....

Having goals is the way we are trained in this society to achieve "success." How often do we hear people say, "By the time I'm 45 I want to be financially secure, own my own house, and have a comfortable retirement to look forward to." But goals can be limiting. What if something else was meant to unfold for us that would give us a lot more joy and happiness but we blocked it because we had a specific goal? When we let go of our rigid attachment to goals, our lives can unfold organically without us controlling the outcome. Of course we will still have projects we work on and things we work towards with intention. The trick is to hold onto them lightly and to keep feeling out what wants to happen rather than pushing for a desired outcome with grim determination. This takes far less energy and requires only that we are present in each moment and respond to what is set before us.

Control vs. surrender...

The opposite of control is surrender. When we surrender, we trust that God will attend to our needs and guide our lives. It is an act of faith and courage where all we need to do is to respond appropriately to what is going on. In this place, the need to control feelings may diminish too. We become spontaneous, expressing ourselves as we are moved to, maybe even with some "reckless abandon!" When was the last time you jumped into a fountain just for the joy of it?

Let us be clear that surrender does not mean disempowerment. In fact, it is the opposite. The surrendered person is extremely empowered. They are acting on their internal gut feelings and paying attention to the cues of the universe around them, without preference. The energy that was used for control can now be used for creativity and well-being, rendering the person more available for the bounty of life's blessings.

When we give up control we no longer resist life. We play in the unknown, where miracles can happen at any moment and our life can unfold just the way it wants to for us to get our lessons and insights gently and completely. In reality, nothing is ever against us. We are always getting what we need in order to become more awakened.

> *"The Kingdom of God is within, now, in everyone. Right now. You have forgotten how to access it because you have gotten lost in the mind. The mind keeps telling you how you are going to be safe, secure and how you can predict life. But you are not safe, you are not secure, and there is no predictability. The moment you accept this totally, here and now, you are in that indescribable inner state."* —Paul Lowe, *In Each Moment*

Examples:

I've been leading yoga retreats for a few years now. When I first started I definitely had an agenda of how I expected people to behave. I would get quite upset if some students didn't join a class segment and would actively encourage them to participate fully. I met with a lot of resistance. So now I allow people to do whatever they need without needing to activate my desire to control them. Everything flows more smoothly as a result and the participants often comment on the sense of permission that they have, to do just what they feel they need to do.

I once dated a guy who insisted on having everything his own way. He would choose the restaurant we ate at. He would order for both of us and insist that I share the food. I was not "allowed" to drink wine in his presence. I was told to make sure I kept his car spotless while I was in it. The list went on and on. He was never willing to negotiate about anything. Things were either done his way or he would sulk. He was not a happy person, as there would always be a constant barrage of things in his life that upset him. By trying to control the people in his life, he would always end up shutting them out in time. He became a loner with few friends. Eventually he pushed me away too.

My friend Tina got a new dog who quickly became her pride and joy! The first time she left to go on vacation and had to leave the dog in the care of her friend, she gave the friend precise instructions about how to feed the dog, how long it should be walked, where it should sleep, and other such details. While on vacation she worried about the animal and wondered if her instructions were being followed. When she came home to get the dog, she found out that indeed, her careful instructions had not been followed, and her first reaction was one of alarm and anger. But then she saw that her dog was happy and realized that her need to control how her dog was taken care of had been unnecessary and had only caused her to worry while she had been gone.

My friend Valerie recently gave up her yuppie lifestyle and now travels around the country in a van, playing music, writing stories and selling her crafts. Her mother disapproves and recently wrote a letter to her telling about how "emotionally wrought" she was at the thought of her MBA daughter sleeping in a van in a parking lot somewhere. When Valerie received the letter she was hurt, but then saw clearly that it was a control tactic to manipulate her to leave the gypsy life. She recognized a familiar tone of disapproval, meant to induce her to change her behavior. Feeling shamed, she watched her creative energy lessen.

While she did not stop traveling, she did stop writing stories for a while. Then she began to recover her creative self and one day received a profound new awareness that this letter from her mother had given her a direct experience of the negative cycles of control: judgment, shame, disempowerment, and manipulation. With this awareness came intuitive information on how to protect herself against it. She repeated the following affirmation to herself until she felt clear of the guilt and shame: "I affirm to myself that there is nothing wrong with my behavior." Valerie heard another message too, a bigger, more hidden message, "My mother loves me. And I love her too."

Saint Francis had a wonderful way of surrendering control in his daily life of running the monastery. Every time a new monk would show up and want to join the Order he would put them in charge!

> *If you want to make God laugh,*
> *tell her your plans!*

Exercises:

Immediate action:

For one day, consciously let go of wanting to have things your own way. Instead, accept everything that shows up just the way it is, as being sacred to your day's process. See how this feels.

Ongoing Awareness:

Look at control as it shows up in your life. If you catch yourself using your will to affect an outcome, ask yourself if you are disturbing the peace of others by this and check in with yourself to see if it really is appropriate action for your higher good. Notice how it feels when others try to control you.

A mother was worried about her son. He was five years old and had not yet uttered a word. She took him to several doctors who tested him and all pronounced him completely healthy. She was told not to worry, but worry she did.

One day she burned his morning oatmeal, but as she was in a hurry that day, she served it to him anyway. He tasted it, spat it out, and said, "Mother, this tastes just awful! How could you feed me this?"

His mother was overcome with joy. "You can talk! But why didn't you say anything before this?"

He looked at her with some puzzlement, then said, "Well, everything's been alright up till now!"

DANCING IN THE LIGHT

This section invites us to look at fulfilling our purpose here on earth, exploring what fills our hearts with joy and satisfies us at a deep soul level. We get to look at how our unique gifts can serve our fellow humans for the benefit of all and for the fulfillment of the Divine Will.

19

What makes my heart sing?

Puts us on our true path to bliss

I gave up a lucrative career in advertising in order to live my passion. Actually, it took me a while to discover what that was for me, so during the process I traveled the world, because I knew I enjoyed that, and waited to see what would unfold. Eventually I was led to practicing yoga and realized that what really gave me pleasure was sharing the yoga tools I had learned with others. That's why I wrote this book and that's why I teach and produce videos. When I'm working on these things, my heart is filled with a joy and a feeling of complete peace. It's as though I'm being guided and the work is coming through me, not from me. I may not have made the same amount of money as I would have done had I followed the typical career path, but that pales into insignificance compared with the pleasure that teaching yoga has given me over the years.

When our heart is singing, it's God's way of telling us that what we are doing is a valuable contribution to the world. Sharing our gifts is what makes us happy, and God wants us to feel happy and fulfilled, allowing us our fullest expression of the Divine. Happiness is also infectious—it is a way of spreading our love to others. When we do our heart's delight, we feel alive and vital. Energy pours through us in such a bountiful way that we have so much more of ourselves to share.

Creativity and illumination are the same thing. They help us to tap into reserves of energy and joy that defy the norm and inspire everyone around us. It is noticeable that people thus illumined march to the beat of their own drum and possess a youthfulness that defies their age. Consider here the many impressionist painters of nineteenth-century France who lived to a ripe old age, inspired as they were with Divine creative energy flowing through them!

Closer to home here in California, I read a newspaper article about Robert Mondavi, the great wine-maker, still working long hours in his late eighties, still passionate about wine and the Arts, and still feeling like he has lots to learn. When it comes to aliveness and energy, let's not forget rockers Tina Turner and Mick Jagger, still performing and touring in their sixties!

What's the excuse?...

When we are younger, we spend a lot of time following our heart. We play, dance, sing, travel, and spend free time exploring the world and our place within it. Maybe we choose a career that resonates with us deeply, even though it may not pay well. Then, as we grow older, something begins to change. Perhaps we have children or financial pressures that require us to get a better-paying and more stressful job. We start to feel bogged down, tired by life, in a rut. Our hobbies or work passions tend to fall away from our everyday experience. We make the excuse that we are too busy for them. We don't have enough money. Or we don't have any friends to join us in our pursuits. Is this really true, or are we making excuses for ourselves? Sometimes we allow our "shoulds" and fears to block our bliss. We think we "should" be working hard and making money, or we are afraid that we will be judged for pursuing what some people may call an "adolescent dream." While writing this I suddenly realized I hadn't played tennis for two years—and I love to play tennis! I immediately called a few friends and made a date to play.

Many of my women friends say that they have devoted themselves for many years to their families and no longer know who they are and what they really want. They no longer know what makes their heart sing. One friend told me she had realized this recently and is now enjoying a process of re-discovering herself. She is exploring new opportunities and revisiting old hobbies to see what brings her happiness now. She says to me that the very experience of this exploration is a joy. We can all do this. We can all re-invent ourselves at any time, letting go of the excuses and finding a way to live our dreams. It all begins with the intention.

Once we have a clear intention of developing an intimate relationship with our joy, we can summon the help of our intuition to help us navigate this field of bliss. We can take stock of what leaves us feeling juiced-up, alive, energized, and inspired, and notice which activities we are intuitively drawn to. We can discover our talents, our God-given gifts that are asking to be utilized and enjoyed by doing what comes naturally. At the same time we can visualize ourselves expressing our talents and then watch for synchronicities that may appear to support that activity. We can get our guidance by paying attention to the signposts that life presents us with—doors that magically open for us, the feedback of others, and how we ourselves feel about what we are doing. We can use these as clues to guide us along our path, noticing above all that which brings the most sense of aliveness into our lives. It's also useful to notice what it is that depletes our energy. When we know without a doubt what is not our bliss, we can more easily detect what is.

> *"It is very rare to come across a happy man. And only the happy man is sane; the unhappy man is insane."* —Osho

Happy hobbies...

Following our bliss may not always be a career decision. It can be that our heart's delight is a hobby such as ballroom dancing or bird watching that gives us tremendous pleasure quite separate from our work life. Nonetheless, this hobby needs to be pursued for us to feel fulfilled. We should never deny ourselves our heart's delight. That would be a sure way to stunt our creativity. The only regrets people on their deathbeds have are that they did not do more to follow their passion. They never seem to regret not spending more time at the office!

Sometimes we need to summon our courage and take a risk

in order to pursue our dreams fully. Risk-taking is a great way to test our willingness to experience our fullness. Are we prepared to make a fool of ourselves for God? Are we prepared to fail?

I have a friend who dreams of being a stand-up comic. She is honing her skills by sharing her talent with the hardest group, her friends and peers, at many social gatherings. Now she is gearing up to take her act to the local comedy clubs. This excites her and gives her a great opportunity to unleash her creative genius. Yet the risk she is taking here is that she won't make people laugh and could fall flat on her face with the wrong crowd. Still, she is courageous and willing to risk making a fool of herself by following her dreams.

Many of us feel that lack of money is an obstacle in pursuing our dreams. Is this really so or is it another excuse that we concoct in our heads? Let's say that we had a terminal illness and needed $50,000 for an operation that would save our lives. Could we raise the money? Many people have—when their lives depended on it! What if we put the same kind of energy and commitment into the joyful expression of our gifts?

A passionate sense of purpose has been shown to be the number one cause of happiness in human beings! So rather than waiting for "one day" to come, we can move in the direction of our heart's delight, bringing as much as possible of our passion into our life now. For example, if we want to write a book but think we don't have time, we can discipline ourselves to write for 30 minutes a week. If we want to travel but think we don't have enough money to do a big trip, we can go camping on the weekend. Breaking our big dream up into small action steps that we do with commitment and consistency is a sure-fire way of producing change in our lives.

Examples:

My friend Melissa is married to a man who does not enjoy the great outdoors like she does. When she realized she was spending far too many weekends at home in the city and not getting out into nature enough, she decided to take matters into her own hands. She joined two hiking groups and bought her own hiking guide-book for the nearby mountains. When she's not doing a group hike, she calls her friends and organizes her own. She reports that she is feeling far more balance and joy in her life now as a result.

My mother loves to sing. When she was young, she used to perform in musicals for amateur dramatic groups. She loved this and indeed, met my father through her singing. However, her second husband was jealous of the attention that was given to my mother when she sang, so he forbade her to perform. She honored his wish but it ate her up inside. She was denying a God-given talent that had no more outlet. This left her feeling quite resentful and bitter. Eventually the relationship disintegrated and when it did, my mother returned to her singing and became a much happier person again.

My friend Kelly feels that her heart's delight is always inside of her, no matter what she is doing. For her it is about connecting with her source, that place of serenity that is always present within us, even while she is washing the dishes or doing the ironing. In this way she has the ability to shift the stresses and chores of daily life into bliss.

A male friend of mine has a passion for singing. There is only one problem—he has a terrible voice! His cat runs and hides whenever he opens his mouth! So he has taken to singing in his car, really loudly! He says it makes him so happy!

Exercises:

Immediate action:

Imagine you have a year to live. What is it you truly would want to do in that year that would allow you to be the most content and fulfilled? Look at the list and then write down a schedule of how you can begin to incorporate these activities into your life.

Ongoing awareness:

Be aware of those things that make you feel truly happy, fulfilled, and energized. See if you can continue to add into your life anything else from your original list. As your exploration continues, update the list. If they are things that require travel or planning such as scuba diving or skiing, work out a way for yourself to do this, maybe a budget, holiday schedule, etc. Sometimes even the thought of doing what we really enjoy helps us to feel happier. Take baby steps if need be. If you've always wanted to drive racing cars, start with go-karts. If you want to be a ballerina, take dance lessons. If you knew you could not fail, which dream would you pursue right now?

Grandma Jones was 89 years old when her husband died. As she was blind and unable to take care of herself, the day came when she needed to be moved into a nursing home. As she maneuvered her walker towards the elevator, the nurse gave her a description of her room. "I love it!" she exclaimed with the enthusiasm of a child.

"But Mrs. Jones, you haven't seen the room yet!"

"That doesn't have anything to do with it," she replied. "Happiness is something you decide on ahead of time. Whether I like my room or not is not about how the furniture is arranged, it's about how I arrange my mind. And I've already decided to love it!"

20

How can I serve?

Brings us into alignment with God's Will

I have always been somewhat of a hedonist. An insatiable urge to travel to exotic places when I was younger exposed me to the beauty of the planet and the joys of pleasure-seeking. I loved to scuba-dive, hike up mountains, receive massages, and travel off the beaten track.

Of course, I couldn't afford to do these things. So necessity being the father of invention, I got creative. I worked as a hostess at a Club Mediterranean in Morocco and learned to ride and sail. I worked behind the bar in a Swiss Hotel so I could ski for a season. I wanted to go to Africa and do a safari so I went to Durban in South Africa and got a job serving pizza to make the money for the trip. Then, as money was still tight, I hitchhiked alone around Southern Africa to see the sights. To receive more massage, I went to massage school, learned how to do it myself, and was then able to trade treatments.

Somehow it all worked out.

I mention all this because recently the pursuit of selfish pleasure has begun to shift for me. The desire and drive to go out and do all these activities is diminishing and something else is taking its place that is ultimately far more satisfying and in line with my purpose on this planet. What's happening is, I am feeling more content now to just stay home and teach and do my work as a spiritual coach rather than dash around the world. It's as though I got all those external desires out of my system and now they are just falling away. In their place is...nothing. Just day-to-day taking care of myself and seeing what shows up to do. I'm available, without having to make anything happen. And the joy I receive from being available to share the teachings and tools of yoga with others is immense.

Karma yoga...

Karma yoga can be defined as service to others without attachment to outcome. It involves the dedication of all work as an offering to God, with no thought of personal reward. By renouncing the fruits of one's action, the action becomes unselfish, expanding the heart, and helping to lessen the grip of the ego. Karma yoga in the form of serving the community is encouraged by many of the ashrams where yoga is taught and practiced. Students help with the cooking, the cleaning, the gardening, or any other task that is required.

In our materialistic modern world the idea of karma yoga may seem hard to grasp, especially the renouncing of outcome. It goes somewhat contrary to our idea of goal achievement and "getting ahead." Instead, this yoga teaches us to give for the joy of giving without any attachment, almost like giving someone a birthday gift and letting go of any preconceived idea about what the recipient does with the gift.

In my own life I have come to learn that all workshops I may host take on a life of their own and that I am not responsible for the individual experience of the students. My job is to show up and be as present and available as possible. What the students do with the information shared and the environment provided is not my concern. In this place I always offer up the workshop experience to God in a prayer that "Divine Will be done." This helps me to not take it personally in the event that a student does not enjoy something about the program. If it is in my control to do something about it I do. If not, I work on releasing my own attachment to pleasing everyone, knowing that I come from a place of pure heart in my willingness to be of service to the best of my ability.

An instrument of love...

A Course in Miracles says that our only real pleasure comes from doing God's Will. It doesn't matter what it is. No job is too big or too small for God to use. Not everyone has a grand and spectacular calling. It could be that our purpose is to raise a family and live sweetly in a quiet suburban neighborhood or to be the friendly restaurant waitress offering hot coffee and good cheer to the weary.

No matter what we do, we can make it our ministry. Every person has the opportunity to bring more love into the universe.

There are countless opportunities for demonstrating love in action, particularly with our immediate family. If we are a parent we can choose to experience great joy in the responsibility of raising our children as well as we can. Serving our own aging parents is a wonderful opportunity to break old family patterns and come from a fresh, new place of love without agenda. My friend Kriya goes back to her parents' home and takes great pleasure in cooking and cleaning for her elderly mother. Not only does her mother really appreciate it but Kriya feels uplifted too. The choice to be used as an instrument of love is a choice of personal empowerment.

Service is selfish...

In some ways, service is the ultimate act of selfishness. Why? Because we feel huge amounts of pleasure, fulfillment, and joy when we do the Divine Will. I know when I'm serving because I feel energy coursing through me that was not there before. I feel energized and uplifted from the experience, no matter what it was. For example, when I lead jnana yoga classes, where we sit for two hours and just talk, at the end of class I feel like I just had a stimulating physical work-out, such is the effect of the energy flowing through me. I take that feeling as a sign that I am serving God and that God has worked through me using me as an instrument.

Letting our light shine...

If we are not yet clear on how we can serve and what our

purpose truly is, we can go into meditation and ask God to reveal it to us. If we are still unclear, we can ask our friends what they think we are good at and see if their feedback inspires us. We can ask them how well they see us to be using our God-given gifts to complete our life's mission. Or we can ask ourselves, if money were no problem, what would we be doing with our lives? Whatever our activity, we can ask that it be used to bless the world. As we open up our hearts more and more, we are moved in the directions where we are supposed to go. Our gifts well up inside of us and flow of their own accord. We accomplish effortlessly.

Once we surrender up our lives to God, divine power can start to flow freely through us. We were all meant to shine and manifest the glory of God that is within us. As we let our light shine, we unconsciously give permission to others to do the same. Once we remember what we're here to do, we can go full speed ahead with our purpose, leading a life of fulfillment and contentment.

> *"May God's will be done" is the same as saying "May I become the best I'm capable of being."*
> —Marianne Williamson, *Return to Love*

Examples:

Mother Teresa was a karma yogi. That is, she served her people completely without any attachment to an outcome. The poorest, sickest people from the Calcutta streets would find her. She embraced everyone. She knew most of her charges would die. She just loved them as she would have done Jesus. Hers was a life of fulfillment and completed purpose.

My psychic healer friend writes for a health magazine. He says that a few days before he is to write his monthly article, he can feel the energy pulse through him and the excitement rising. When he feels this energy flow inspiring him, he feels that this is a sure pointer that he is doing God's Will.

One teacher of mine spent quite a lot of time volunteering at a hospice. He was given the prickliest patients to visit. One time he went to see a lady who was dying of lung cancer. She sat surrounded by friends and family as she lay dying.

"Whaddya want?' the lady yelled as he approached.

"I only want to know how I can serve you," he replied gently, as she scowled at him skeptically.

"Well, you can start by giving me that packet of cigarettes over there," she snarled, not thinking for a moment that he would comply. To her surprise, her visitor picked up the pack and offered her the cigarettes, despite the disapproving looks from the family and friends gathered. She softened and began to talk. "You are the only one who has honored a dying lady's wish," she said with tears in her eyes. She died later that day. But she died having had her free will honored one last time.

> *"No joy can equal the joy of serving others."*
> —Sai Baba

Exercises:

Immediate Action:

Ask your friends and colleagues how you can serve them without second guessing them or trying to fix them in some way. We do not know what it is that they need if we don't ask! Asking how you can serve and then following through is an act of unconditional love to a high degree.

Ongoing awareness:

Volunteer your services in some way, maybe at a retirement home, animal shelter, or hospice. Or ask your elderly neighbor if they need help with the shopping. Share your good cheer with those less fortunate than yourself. Notice what is to be learned from seeing how other people deal with their own unique challenges.

Add the question "How can I serve?" to your prayers. Pay attention to what shows up. Surrender your life to God and ask to be used as an instrument of peace.

SUCCESS

He has achieved success who has lived well,
laughed often and loved much;

who has enjoyed the trust of pure women,
the respect of intelligent men
and the love of little children;

who has filled his niche and accomplished his task;

who has left the world better than he found it,
whether by an improved poppy,
a perfect poem, or a rescued soul;

who has never lacked appreciation of earth's beauty
or failed to express it;

who has always looked for the best in others
and given them the best he had;

whose life was an inspiration;

whose memory is a benediction.

—Bessie A. Stanley

Afterword

Our process of unfoldment continues endlessly. To facilitate further inquiry another set of questions is being prepared which will form the basis of the next book: *20 More Questions for Enlightened Living.* Here are a few of the topics that will be discussed.

What's the fear?

We look at our instinctual fear and compare it to the fears that we manufacture in our heads. Strategies for coping with fear will be presented. The concept of positive and negative polarities will be introduced along with techniques for clearing our constant swings from one polarity to another.

What's the assumption?

This chapter examines our tendencies to create scenarios in our minds that have no bearing on reality. We see with some amusement the trouble these assumptions can get us into!

What's the story?

Here we see how the continued telling of our story keeps us identified with it and unable to break free from our past and our pain.

What's different?

This question invites us to look at our routines and habits and to find fresher, newer ways of being in the world that lead to more spontaneity and joy.

How can I feel that I am "enough?"

This question is about lack: the feeling that we lack something, need to do more, or be a different way in order to be loved.

Instead we find ways of raising self-esteem and embracing self-love so that we get it that our presence is enough.

How can we celebrate?

The ultimate way to not take life too seriously is to celebrate all of it! The ups and the down, the smiles the frowns. We celebrate the process each and every step of the way!

Who am I?

We look at ways to drop into a deeper sense of presence and Truth with this ultimate question.

We explore ways to drop into the neutral mind, beyond duality, beyond the pull of opposite polarities. This involves being neither attracted nor repulsed, as we surrender our desires and fears. Instead we aim to be in the "stateless state," the "clear light of the void," present yet without attributes. We discover neutrality to be a doorway to a higher level of vibration and consciousness. Life is still experienced, but from a more detached state.

We explore the statement, " I am That," an affirmation of the highest order that starts to dissolve the human condition. What happens when we continually affirm this statement?

We begin the practice of "neti neti," which means "not this, not that." We start the process of dropping our identification with feelings and emotions. Instead, we feel them and acknowledge them passing through us from the point of view of the neutral witness.

Asking "Who am I?" together with the stripping away of who we are not, leads us to a place beyond the mind where nothing remains to describe the individual being but the true, essential nature of the Self. There is no more sense of separation, just awareness and unity. Life becomes a meditation. The ego is experienced as dissolved and the individual perceived as a cell in the body of God, a unique expression of the oneness of all that is. The word "yoga" in Sanskrit means union and it is this union with oneness that is yoga's ultimate purpose.

*Check out my website at **www.juliatindall.com** to get an early peek at upcoming chapters from the next book!*

The History of Jnana Yoga

The origins of jnana yoga predate written history. Traditionally this Self-inquiry was directed by a spiritual teacher or guru, who personally guided the student into states of higher awareness. Indeed, even after the advent of writing, this yoga was still usually transmitted by word of mouth.

In ancient times traditional jnana yoga was associated with the aesthetic lifestyle and the renunciation of all things material. Living in society was not considered conducive to the process of this Self-inquiry, as it was thought that being part of the material world did not foster an environment for the intensity of practice that was deemed necessary. Moreover, the teachings of jnana yoga were given only to men. Women were considered temptresses that could lead the renunciate off his chosen path. They were excluded from teachings and shunned by jnanis (practitioners of jnana yoga).

Traditional jnana was based on the non-dualistic philosophy of the Advaita Vedanta, the scripture of the Upanishads that states that all is Brahman, or unmanifested God. The practice would often involve the jnani focusing on the question, "Who am I?" by practicing "neti neti," which means "not this, not that." If the practitioner noticed an identification with ego, they may think, "I am not this name/ body/desire." If they noticed a thought they may think, "I am not this thought." If a feeling was observed they might think, "I am not this feeling." With this practice, the jnani would dissolve all belief systems about himself and all identification with ego, body and mind until he became empty enough to merge back his consciousness into the oneness of Creation.

Classical texts

The Bhagavad Gita, which forms a part of the classic Indian epic, the Mahabharata, is one of the classic texts studied by jnanis to aid them in their Self-inquiry. Much of the text focuses on the nature of attachments, the nature of God and the nature of duty. "He whose undertakings are all devoid of desires and selfish purposes and whose actions have been burnt by the fire of knowledge—him the wise call a sage. Having abandoned attachment to the fruits of actions, ever content, depending on nothing, he does not do anything, though engaged in activity." (Chapter 4, verses 19–20) This Holy Scripture is studied to this day by seekers of truth the world over, as a guidepost to timeless wisdom.

Around the seventh century, Shankara, the most important philosopher of Advaita Vedanta, wrote his classic text *Crest Jewel of Discrimination.* In this text Shankara developed the technique of "viveka," or discernment, which involves continuous effort to understand that the real Self is separate from objects of our awareness. Although not much is known about the life of Shankara, his words remain as a precious guide to Self-discovery.

The Yoga Sutras, (verses) commonly thought to have been written by the scholar Patanjali, who lived between the third century B.C. and the third century A.D., describe the system of classical yoga as having eight parts. Two of these parts are called "yamas" (restraints), actions and attitudes to avoid, and "niyamas" (observances), which describe actions and attitudes we can cultivate to bring more ease and peace into our lives. It is these teachings that describe ways of raising our consciousness about how we live that have relevance for jnana yoga practice.

For example, "ahimasa" (non-violence) is the practice of becoming conscious of destructive behavior towards the Self and others. Besides physical violence this yama includes violence of words and thoughts. It involves such things as noticing when we carry shame, guilt and fear, or when we criticize and judge others.

"Satya" (truthfulness) is the practice of being in integrity in all aspects of our lives from telling the truth to being our word.

"Aparigraha" (non-possessiveness) teaches us to live simply and within our means, taking for ourselves only what is necessary and being grateful for our possessions without attachment to them.

"Shauch" (purity) is a complex teaching that encourages us to be of pure intentions and act from the place of a pure heart, selflessly and without ego. It involves the congruity of life, that is, letting the external world reflect the inner, and is also concerned with observing thoughts without judgment or attachment.

"Santosh" (contentment) is about staying in the Now, not dwelling on the past or future, just celebrating the present moment. It invites us to be grateful for what we have, no matter our circumstance, and also to act to the best of our ability in the moment.

"Svadyaya" (study) is the practice of studying holy texts and learning from a teacher, to help stir remembrance of our own latent knowledge and wisdom. The act of reading this book may be considered Svadyaya but the practical exercises described in the book is the practice of jnana.

Patanjali's sutras were brief, yet complex, which underscores the fact that they were written at a time when oral teaching was the norm. For the student to appreciate the richness of the text, it was meant to be studied under the guidance of a teacher.

Yoga moves west

Very little about jnana yoga that has remained with us was written in the centuries preceding the 1800's. Indeed, even great Indian Saints of the last two centuries such as Sri Ramakrishna were not interested in writing anything down. However, their students wrote their words into books such as *The Gospel of Sri Ramakrishna.* Ramakrishna lectured extensively on traditional jnana yoga, based on the teachings of Vedantic literature, and inspired many devotees to come to his ashram. One of his disciples was Swami Vivekenanda.

In the late nineteenth century, with the British firmly established in India, more and more spiritual teachers from the East were being sought after and studied by westerners hungry for Truth. Swami Vivekenanda was invited to come on a lecture tour of England at the turn of the twentieth century. His lectures were recorded and made into books, one of which is called *Jnana Yoga.* Filled with wonderful anecdotes and stories, Swami Vivekananda invited his audience to question the way they looked at reality and dive deeper into Self-Inquiry and fulfill true potential as human beings.

Just a few years later, Swami Yogananda was sent to the west by his guru and established some of the first yoga centers in America. Yogananda was a prolific author and wrote many books on all the different aspects of yoga.

Similarly, Swami Sivananda, born in 1887, was also a prolific writer on yoga, including jnana yoga. His book, *Self-Knowledge* (Divine Life Society, India, 1958), talks about the many ways to become one with Brahman (God). He sent his disciple, Swami Vishnudevananda, to Canada to found the first Sivananda Yoga Center where students could come to learn about all the different aspects of yoga, including raja, bhakti, karma and jnana yoga. Today Sivananda yoga centers are found all over the world.

Bhagavan Sri Ramana Maharshi (1879–1950) was probably the most famous Indian sage of the twentieth century. He was renowned for his saintly life, for the fullness of his Self-realization and for the feelings of deep peace that visitors experienced in his presence. He became Self-realized at the age of 16 and soon after ran away to the holy hill of Arunachala where he remained for the rest of his life. An ashram was built around him. He taught a method of Self-inquiry in which the seeker focuses attention on the I-thought in order to find its source.

One of the disciples at his ashram was H.W.L. Poonja, commonly known as "Papaji." Papaji received his enlightenment at the feet of Ramana and in later life started to share the teachings in Lucknow, India. He died in 1997, but not before helping to enlighten the hundreds of seekers who came from all over the world to his satsang (sitting with the guru).

One of these seekers was Antoinette Varner, later renamed Gangaji. She says that when she looked into his eyes she saw the cosmos. After realizing her true Self, Papaji instructed her to go home and carry his transmission to the west. Today Gangaji holds satsangs throughout the world, as well as in prisons and on video.

No discussion on twentieth-century jnana yoga could be complete without mention of Jiddu Krishnamurti. Born in 1895 in India, Krishnamurti soon became one of the world's greatest philosophical minds. At the age of 16 he was taken to England for further education by his adoptive Mother, who also happened to be president of the Theosophical Society. He was hailed as a "New Messiah," "A World Teacher," and an organization was set up to promote this role. However, Krishnamurti insisted on having no followers, saying that the moment we follow someone we cease to follow Truth, and later disbanded the organization.

Krishnamurti spent more than sixty years giving passionate discourses on the myriad ways in which the human mind turns to self-delusion in its never-ending quest for fulfillment. Although he refused to be categorized, his teachings are essentially about jnana yoga. He encouraged a fierce and relentless Self-inquiry, involving the dismantling of all belief systems and the stripping away of all illusions and delusions. He offered no techniques, doctrines or practices, just the invitation for people to become more attentive, to make their own discoveries. He urged individuals to discover for themselves the experience of meditation and the nature of their thought processes through activating the witness, or silent observer. In this way he led people towards freedom, freedom from limitations so the Self can be realized. He said, "Freedom is pure observation without direction, without fear of punishment and reward." Krishnamurti died in 1986 in Ojai, California. His talks, dialogues and writings have been preserved in seventy books and hundreds of videos and recordings.

Spirituality meets psychology

With the advent of deeper understanding of the functioning of the mind and expansion in the science of psychology in the twentieth century, we can see some changes in the way that jnana yoga has evolved. In *The Synthesis of Yoga,* which first appeared in periodicals in the early twentieth century, Sri Aurobindo wrote extensively about jnana being one of the essential features of his unique integral yoga. He said, "All life is yoga" and formed an ashram in Pondicherry, India, where devotees could live his teachings. He wrote about starting with the mind to go beyond the mind, just as we do in this book. "This pure jnanayoga comes by the intellect, although it ends in the transcendence of the intellect and its workings." (*Synthesis of Yoga,* p. 274)

As Indian gurus and teachers moved west and more and more westerners traveled to India in search of wisdom, the psychology of the west and the spirituality of the east began to merge. Attitudes changed and with the recognition of women as equals in the twentieth century, women, too, began to gravitate towards yoga and were accepted as students.

A new starting place for jnana yoga evolved that made the practice accessible to more people. Rather than beginning with the difficult path of meditating on "neti neti" and "Who am I?" the modern-day student is invited to practice activating witness consciousness and investigating attachments, beliefs and behaviors of the personality, utilizing Sri Aurobindo's philosophy of using the mind to go beyond itself. Students are encouraged to use their everyday experiences to enhance their practice rather than running away from society or living in isolated ashrams.

One of our greatest living jnanis is a woman from South Africa named Leslie Temple-Thurston. Leslie was a painter and a mystic from an early age. Since realizing the truth of her Self, she has dedicated her life to giving darshan (spiritual transmissions) and sharing techniques that she herself used to wake up. Her approach is clear and easy to understand. Although Leslie says her teachings have their roots in Advaita Vedanta, she has expanded these teachings and made them more accessible for western minds. Her processing techniques for clearing the ego/mind are excellent and can be found in her book *Marriage of Spirit* (see Suggested Reading).

Just as Tibetan Buddhism has come to the west and the Dalai Lama has adapted his teachings to have relevance for the western lifestyle, so jnana yoga has evolved in a way that is now accessible to all. Since the 1970's there has been a relative explosion of new age and spiritual books in publication that reflect our culture's appetite for investigation and understanding of both our humanness and our divinity. Many of these books are intrinsically jnana yoga in content, although they have not been labeled as such. Starting with Ram Dass' *Be Here Now,* including *A Course in Miracles,* and more recently *The Four Agreements* by Don Miguel Ruiz, these texts all guide us in ways to raise our awareness and activate our witness consciousness.

Guidelines for Group Facilitation

Gathering together regularly in a group is the most powerful way I have found to work with the information in this book. As a group, we support each other in our process and can quicken each other's healing. For example, someone else's issues may trigger something for us to look at that we otherwise would not have considered. We realize that we are not alone in the issues that confront us and can feel comforted to have this community of friends who are supporting us on our path of self-awareness. This is vitally important, as feeling alone out there in the world is one of the biggest challenges that many of us face. To be surrounded regularly by a group of non-judgmental, like-minded, supportive people is a gift indeed.

Establishing procedures

In my jnana yoga groups we always begin by setting the spiritual mood for the session. After all, it is the context of spirituality that sets a jnana yoga group apart from a plain therapy group. I like to bring everyone into a circle sitting on the floor. If that doesn't work for some people then use chairs, but be close together, knees touching if possible, and holding hands to establish a feeling of intimacy right from the start. As facilitator I bring the group together with a short centering meditation and a prayer. Here is what I say. Please feel free to use the same verbiage, or modify it as you see fit.

"Let's all come together in a comfortable sitting position and close the eyes. Allow the tailbone to drop down into the ground, hooking you into the earth and lean back into your sit-bones. Relax the shoulders, lift the chest slightly to straighten the spine and allow your attention to go to your breath, gaining a sense and an awareness of breath consciousness. On the next exhalation just allow the events of your day to slip softly from your shoulders, melting into the ground

and letting go. Let go of all that has gone before and all that is yet to come and be here now, affirming that this is a time for healing and nurturing and for mending the bond of trust with your God-Self. Take a deep inhalation and lengthen the spine and inhale once more and join in oms."

I lead the group in three om chants. We follow with a prayer that goes something like this:

"Great Spirit, we ask that you bless this gathering tonight and give us the courage to open our hearts and speak our truth. We ask that you imbue our discussion with wisdom and compassion and guide us gently on our path of Self-discovery. We offer up our prayers and invite all your blessings down upon us. Jai Ma" (this means "whoopee God!").

In new groups I start out by welcoming everyone to jnana yoga and introducing myself. I then go around the circle and ask the students to introduce themselves and say why they are here and what it is they are looking for in this group. That way we begin to get a sense of each other, and everyone feels they have already participated, so shyness starts to dissolve.

Next I discuss the guidelines for group participation. First and most important, I get everyone to agree to a condition of confidentiality in order to make the space safe and sacred for our sharing, which is often of a very personal and intimate nature. We agree that everything that is discussed does not leave the room, and there is to be no gossiping or story telling about what goes on here.

Next we talk about commitment to attendance. I like to run my groups in four, six, or eight-week sessions. That way we can invite new people to join us whenever the group opens up again. Having a few weeks in between group sessions allows the students some time to integrate what we have learned.

I allow new students to join us during the first two weeks of a new session, but after that we close the group and no new people can join in. I do this to create more intimacy within the group. When the group is closed and the people get to know each other better, a deeper level of communication and support can occur.

So if a student decides to join, we ask them to commit to showing up each week. If they have a business meeting out of town or are sick and cannot attend, then they commit to calling or emailing me to let me know so I can tell the group why they are absent and also give them the next week's homework. That way they still feel part of our process, even if not physically present.

As far as payment goes, I ask that the students pay in advance for the series. This also helps them to honor their commitment of attendance and honor the work. If a person comes just once and decides it is not for them, I ask for a pro-rated contribution.

Then I talk to the group about how we share. I ask them to focus on talking from personal experiences rather than from the mind's perspective of ideas and thoughts. I encourage them to make "I" statements to help them do this. I also warn them that for the sake of time and in consideration of the group, I will act as hatchet lady, and if anyone is having difficulty in keeping to personal experiences when they talk, I will gently interrupt them and try to bring them down out of their heads and into their hearts as they share. I also encourage them to be brief and to the point so that everyone in group who wants to talk has time.

I tell them that I am not the guru. I do not have all the answers—although I do have some jolly good questions for them! We are here to share our wisdom as a group, and if they have a perspective or experience that is helpful for someone else, then they should please raise their hand and speak. However, when one person is talking, we all listen attentively and do not give commentary until that person is finished. To let us know that they are done talking, the person sharing may just say, "I'm complete," or I will ask them, to be sure, before anyone else chimes in or before I share my perspective with them.

Some groups like to use a "talking stick" of some kind. Actually it could be any object at all. I use a rainstick! The person talking holds the stick and puts it down when they are finished. This procedure really allows the speaker to feel heard and honored. It creates a feeling of respect amongst group members and is particularly important for when we share sensitive issues.

Content

I find it works best to have a theme for each session. This book is conveniently divided up into segments, which lend themselves well for this. If your group is brand new I suggest starting with the first four foundation chapters to get the basics covered and go over terminology, such as the concept of witness consciousness and what we mean by asking *"What's so?"*

Other suggestions for content could be to work with the four attachments, discussing each limb of the monster in turn, or to do a series on clearing up the past. Chapter 12, on love, has plenty of content for at least four weeks' worth of homework. Whichever set you choose, give students the homework of one of the questions to keep in their consciousness for the week. Talk a little about the question you have chosen and how the student might use it to raise awareness. It's always helpful to add a little from your own personal experience, too. Make sure everyone has understood what is being discussed.

Ideally, students will actually read the relevant chapter in the book to give them some more background on the question and to see how it pertains to their lives. The new awareness the students have during the week from the homework will then be used as the focus point for the next meeting.

If you finish discussion of last week's homework and there is still time, open up a place for students to share other challenges, triumphs, or insights that are currently up for them. Or, save some time to do a group meditation before closing.

The first week of running a new group is tricky because you have not yet given the group any homework. This is a good time to go over the principal aims of jnana yoga and introduce students to its history. I then like to ask each person in turn to talk a little about where they are currently challenged in their lives. This helps people to get to know each other and begins to open the arena for discussion. Then you can talk about the theme chosen for the series and go on to discuss the homework.

Facilitator challenges

Over the years I have run into a few challenges in facilitating group dynamics. For example, there are some people who love to give advice. The word "should" often pops up in their speech. When I hear this happening a lot with a certain person I jump in and ask them to speak from their own experience, rather than repeating things they have read in books or what their mother may have told them. Sometimes they are unable to do that and just remain quiet. I often find that habitual advice-givers will not stay in the group, as their cup is possibly a little too full in order for them to really learn.

Some people love to ramble on and on in great Technicolor detail about every facet of their story. Not only is this boring to listen to for other group members but it's also a good indication that the person is talking from a place of mind rather than an experience of the heart. One trick here is to give people a time limit. I sometimes use an egg timer! When their time to speak has run out I invite them to get to the point quickly or we will move on to someone else! This often helps them to dive into the heart of the matter where they can share their deepest truth and be vulnerable, so real transformation can then take place.

Some people tend to dominate the group when it is a free-for-all style of sharing, and others often remain quiet. A technique here is to go around the circle from time to time and ask everyone to give their perspective on a certain issue or question. That way even the shyest people are encouraged to speak and can be heard and supported by the group, and the more talkative people get to practice active listening!

The close

Just before we close our group I ask group members if there is anyone they know in need of healing or support. Students will throw into the circle names of friends and relatives. We imagine them in the center of our circle and send them our healing energy as a group. If a student who is present is not feeling well we invite them to lie down in the center of the circle so we can send them our healing energy. This type of prayer is very powerful and we have often heard about the positive effects it has had on people.

Next, I invite us all to hold hands and close our eyes. Then I say something like this: *"Just begin to let everything settle down. Relax into your sit-bones and allow the attention once again to draw to the breath. Take a moment to absorb all the love and support that's available for you here in this group. Drink it in. Feel fully how it is to be here right now, as part of this circle. Take a deep inhalation, lengthen the spine, and inhale once more, and we'll join in 'oms.'"*

(We all chant om three times.)

"I'd like to thank all of you for being here tonight and sharing your yoga, your wisdom, and your energy. I remind you that true gains come in a personal practice, so play with the homework, value the yoga, and above all, honor yourselves. And may the rest of your week be filled with joy, love, light, and delight. Namaste."

(We all make the gesture of namaste, with the hands in prayer position in front of the chest.)

Building community

One of the great opportunities of forming a jnana yoga group is that of building up a conscious community. To foster this, we have a potluck supper before group, and tea and desserts afterwards, so students have some time to socialize and get to know each other outside the formal group process. This is a great way to establish friendships and continue to enjoy the group energy. What often ends up happening is that students get together on a regular basis outside of our weekly jnana meetings and continue to build on the friendship and intimacy they have found in the group.

Suggested Reading

Here are some books that I have read, along with my comments!

The Classics

Anonymous. ***Gospel of Sri Ramakrishna: Abridged edition,*** **trans. Swami Nikhilananda. New York: Ramakrishna Vivekananda Center, 1988.** A diary of a devotee's experiences around this great master in the late 1800's. Comprehensive and full of spiritual truths, yet a little heavy going to read at times.

Anonymous. ***The Song of God (Bhagavad Gita).*** **South Africa: The Chiltern Yoga Trust, 1984.** The Bhagavad Gita is the Bible of the Hindus. This timeless classic can be read in 3 hours, yet it takes a lifetime to absorb its deeper meanings. I recommend finding a class with a qualified teacher to guide you in understanding it. There are many different commentaries published on the verses. I find this one particularly clear and easy to follow. The commentary is written by Swami Venkatesha, a student from the lineage of Swami Sivananda.

Anonymous. ***The Upanishads Vol. 1–4,*** **trans. Swami Nikhilananda. New York: Ramakrishna Vivekananda Center, 1994.** Poetic and profound, these ancient texts are hard to understand, yet should be read at least once by every serious jnani, if only to absorb the energies of enlightenment that are still transferred from page to reader.

Osborne, A. ***Ramana Maharshi and the Path of Self-Knowledge.*** **York Beach, ME: Samuel Weiser Inc., 1970.** A description of the life and times of Ramana Maharshi, the great modern day saint. Excerpts from dialogues with Ramana are included here. Fascinating!

Sri Nisargadatta Maharaj. ***I am That, Talks with Sri Nisargadatta Maharaj,*** **trans. Maurice Frydman. Durham, NC: Acorn Press, 1982.** Transcripts of over 100 talks that Sri Maharaj gave to devotees during the first part of the twentieth century. I suggest reading this more for the energy behind the words than for any techniques to be gleaned. This book will drive your mind crazy! And that's the point...

Swami Prabhavananda, et al. ***Shankara's Crest Jewel of Discrimination,*** **trans. Christopher Isherwood. Vedanta Press, 1970.** The seventh-century Hindu mystic Shankara speaks clearly about the nature of the Self and the difference between maya and Brahman. Easier to understand than the Upanishads or the Gita, it is a good introductory book into classic vedantic philosophy, written by a great saint who experienced Truth.

Swami Satchidananda. ***The Yoga Sutras of Patanjali.*** **Integral Yoga Distribution, 1990.** The classic treatise on raja yoga translated from the 2300-year-old Indian text. Much studied by yoga schools to this day, many of the observances and recommendations proposed by Patanjali cross over into the realm of jnana yoga.

Vivekananda, S. ***Jnana-Yoga.*** **New York: Ramakrishna-Vivekananda Center, 1955.** Taken from Swami Vivekanandas's lecture tour of Europe in the late nineteenth century, the languaging and thought processes are dated and hard to follow. However if you can get over that, there are many gems of truth hidden within these pages.

Contemporary Mystics

Anonymous. ***A Course in Miracles.*** **Tiburon, CA: Foundation for Inner Peace, 1975.** This is a channeled book that is essentially A Course in Jnana Yoga. Much favored by study groups, the material here is powerful and rich. However, many people including myself find the style long-winded and laborious. It lost my interest before I could get through all of the 1,000+ pages...

Gangaji. ***You are That.*** **Novato, CA: Gangaji Foundation, 1996.** Transcripts of satsang interviews with Gangaji. The simplicity of her message is profound and goes straight to the heart. She invites us to be still, to stop, and let Presence be. Catch her satsangs if she comes to your town—or at least get one on video.

Krishnamurti, J. ***The First and Last Freedom.*** **San Francisco: Harper, 1954.** A wealth of wisdom, this book takes the form of questions presented to this modern mystic and his responses. Don't be put off by the awkward style—the richness of the wisdom here is worth the effort!

Lowe, P. *In Each Moment*. Vancouver, BC: Looking Glass Press, 1998. A clear, easy-to-follow guide to becoming more awake from one of the most gifted spiritual teachers of our modern day. Highly recommended.

Osho. *The Tantra Experience*. India: Rebel Publishing House, 1978. I love this book! Easy to read, written in contemporary, clear language by Osho, the Indian mystic known as the great communicator. This book is so about freedom. It opens my heart and liberates my soul. Can't recommend it highly enough!

Poonja, H.W. L. *Wake up and Roar*. Ed. Eli Jaxon-Bear. Novato: Gangaji Foundation, 1992. Taken from satsang questions to "Papaji," this book provides the reader with wonderful ways to answer the question "Who am I?"

Sri Aurobindo. *The Synthesis of Yoga*. Pondicherry, India: Sri Aurobindo Ashram, 1971. A comprehensive 860+ pages on the value of yoga in our daily world. Not for the meek, this is an intellectual book with many references to the Upanishads and the Gita. Heavy going.

Swami Sivananda. *May I answer that?* International Sivananda Yoga Vedanta Center. A compilation from various published works of Swami Sivananda. Questions and answers that deal with common doubts and concerns of the spiritual aspirant.

Temple-Thurston, L. *The Marriage of Spirit*, Santa Fe, NM: Corelight Publications, 2000. Highly, highly recommended!!! Leslie is a fully-realized modern-day jnani who offers straightforward and down-to-earth ways of processing our hidden blocks and learning to identify more fully with our witness. I particularly recommend the squares processing technique.

Tolle, E. *The Power of Now*. Novato, CA: New World Library, 1999. Mr. Tolle offers portals to our awakening. He suggests we need to pay more attention and become more present and we will drop into an experience of Presence. It worked for him.....

Yogananda, P. *Autobiography of a Yogi*. Los Angeles: Self-Realization Fellowship, 1946. Incredible story of the life of a modern mystic in twentieth-century India. It takes the reader to meet mythical beings such as Babaji in the heart of the Himalayas, and also chronicles Yogananda's relationship with his guru and personal spiritual adventure. Easy to read and heart-warming. This book helped to wake me up. Highly recommended.

Related helpful reading

Campbell, S. *Getting Real.* Novato, CA: New World Library, 2001. A wonderful, practical guide to becoming more authentic! Complete with guided exercises to practice in every-day life, this is a great book for becoming more conscious about ourselves and how we behave in our world.

Christensen, A. *Yoga of the Heart.* New York: Daybreak Books, 1998. A sweet book that takes the teachings of Patanjali's sutras and applies them to our everyday world.

IsanaMada. *A Call to Greatness*. San Francisco, CA: Dhyana Press, 1994. A very good guide to becoming more conscious and fulfilling our true potential as humans. Great exercises and information.

Matthews. A. *Being Happy.* Singapore: Media Masters, 1998. I liked this book. Fun to read with lots of cool cartoons, this little book is also packed with wisdom. It's light yet deep.

Ram Dass. *Be Here Now*. New York: Random House, 1971. The book that opened up so many people when it came out in the early 70's… a classic for our times…highly recommended.

Ruiz, Don M. *The Four Agreements*. Amber-Allen Publishers, 1997. Shamanic teacher Don Miguel Ruiz exposes self-limiting beliefs and presents a simple and effective code of personal conduct learned from his Toltec ancestors. Easy to read and a good adjunct to jnana yoga.

Williamson, M. *A Return to Love*. New York: Harper Collins, 1992. A modern classic, this book opened my heart. Based on *A Course in Miracles,* Marianne brings those teachings to life in an easy-to-understand format. I read this book whilst stuck in a rural Chinese airport in a rainstorm. Yet the Truth contained in these pages pulled me into a state of bliss!

Glossary of Terms

Sanskrit Words and Their Meanings:

Advaita Vedanta: The philosophy of non-duality, the doctrine that nothing exists except spirit.

Darshan: The transmission of spiritual love and divine blessings from guru to participant.

Jnana: Knowledge or wisdom.

Jnana yoga: The practice of inquiring into the nature of ourselves with the intention of seeing the Truth of our being.

Jnani: A practitioner of jnana yoga; an enlightened one who knows the Self.

Maya: The illusory world.

Neti neti: Not this, not that; meaning I am not identifying with this illusion of life.

Satsang: A gathering to share spiritual love and receive divine blessings, normally in the presence of a guru.

Sutras: Threads or verses.

Vedanta: The name of different schools of philosophy founded on the teachings of the Upanishads. Concerned with Self-inquiry.

Viveka: Discrimination between true and false.

Yoga: Union; more specifically, union with God.

English Terms:

Duality: Divided in two, a term used for describing our world, reflecting its nature of opposites.

Ego: The separate self, the false identity, the conditioned personality which perceives itself as separate from the whole.

Enlightenment: An all-encompassing perception of non-separation.

Grace: A force of divine love, healing and support, which flows to us, especially when we pray for it.

Neutral observer (witness): The part of us that is able to perceive without judgment the conditioned personality being acted out.

Polarity: The opposition formed by negatively and positively charged attributes.

self, the: The small self, the ego/personality.

Self, the: The authentic, eternal immortal beingness that we all are.

Self-inquiry: The practice of looking at consciousness.

Self-realization: Permanently actualizing direct knowledge of the Self.

Shadow: The unconscious side of the ego.

About the Author

Julia Tindall is a practicing yoga instructor of hatha, jnana, and tantra yoga. She is also a massage therapist, alchemical hypnotherapist, and international workshop leader. Along with yoga, Julia conducts workshops on other topics such as healing shame and grief. She leads yoga vacations around the world to exotic locations such as Bali, Costa Rica, Mexico and Hawaii. Julia is the producer of many acclaimed yoga videos, including the world's first Partner Yoga video and a television series of half-hour yoga practices. She lives in Sacramento, California.

If you would like more information on Julia's retreats, workshops, or videos, please contact her at 916-486-4620 or email yogajules@aol.com.

Website: www.juliatindall.com

Videotapes, Audiocassettes, and CDs

by Julia Tindall

SAFE AND SENSIBLE VIDEOS TO LEARN FROM AND ENJOY

A1 STANDING WAVE YOGA FLOOR SERIES – This soft and gentle practice helps students to get grounded in the basics of yoga. The focus is on breathing into each asana with conscious awareness, rather than efforting the poses with muscle. The series is practiced entirely on the floor to allow the student to surrender deeply and let go of tension. Suitable for everyone. 1 hour, 15 minutes.

A2 HATHA YOGA ANIMAL SERIES – Safe and slow, yet challenging series for the beginner to intermediate student. This one hour video begins with a breath practice and moves on with the animal series of asanas for spinal flexibility and hip opening, leaving the student feeling refreshed and revitalized for the day.

A3 PARTNER YOGA – Enjoy yoga with a friend! This lighthearted and fun video guides you through a variety of poses where your partner helps you to open your body, gently and joyfully!

A4 BEGINNERS' T'AI CHI – This user-friendly one hour practice begins with an easy-to-follow warm-up routine and continues with the first section of the T'ai Chi Chuan short form demonstrated step-by-step. Filmed from the back as well as the front for ease of learning.

A5 SWEDISH MASSAGE – From toes to head, follow Julia as she guides you through a full-body Swedish oil massage. 1 hour, 15 minutes.

PRICE: Videos A1–A5 are $25 each plus $3 shipping and handling.

HALF-HOUR VIDEOS FROM JULIA'S HATHA YOGA TV SHOW

B1 SHOULDER OPENING SERIES – This set is perfect for opening the shoulder and neck areas. It can be done on the floor or on a chair—great for tense office workers!

B2 DOG AND PIGEON SERIES – This video focuses on opening the hips with variations in pigeon pose and stretching the spine with dog pose.

B3 SUN SALUTATION SET – This set begins with a standing shoulder opener sequence and is followed by a slow flowing sun salutation set with variations. More vigorous—guaranteed to wake you up!

B4 SEATED STRADDLE, CAMEL AND LOTUS PREPARATION SET – This series is mostly done in the seated position. Opens the groin, back and hips.

B5 SEATED SERIES – The perfect set for opening and strengthening the upper back and preventing shrinkage of the spine! A challenging seated set that really works.

B6 STANDING STRADDLE SERIES AND PSOAS OPENER SET – This video focuses on hamstrings, psoas (for lower back integrity) and spine. Much of it is done in the inverted standing position.

B7 FROG AND COBRA SERIES – A nice easy set perfect for beginners or for those who want to open their upper back gently. Includes many backbends done in prone position.

B8 YOGA FOR THE ABS – A fun, eclectic set that concentrates on strengthening the abdominal muscles.

PRICE: Videos B1–B8 are $15 each plus $3 shipping and handling.

"Thanks for the yoga video—you did a GREAT job on it! Even I can follow it! I love your reminders to continue deep abdominal breathing, keep the spine straight...and relax!!" Donna, Fortuna, CA

AUDIOCASSETTES FOR HOME PRACTICE

C1 STANDING WAVE YOGA PRONE SERIES – Same practice as the Floor Series video. A gentle, easy beginner set practiced entirely on the floor.

C2 ANIMAL SERIES YOGA – This one hour tape is similar to the Animal Series Yoga video in content. It covers cat, cow, dog, pigeon, cobra and fish poses performed in a flowing manner using the asanas to open the body. Beginner to intermediate.

C3 BEGINNERS' YOGA – Based on the Sivananda teaching style, this tape includes eye and neck exercises as well as the more vigorous sun salute.

C4 CREATIVE VISUALIZATION – Enjoy a magic carpet ride to your place of sanctuary to meet your inner guidance (25 minutes). On the second side is a seated, healing meditation. (18 minutes).

PRICE: Audiocassettes are $10 plus $1 shipping and handling.

"I love your yoga tape—your voice and manner are so relaxing!"
Victoria Morse, Sacramento, CA

CD

D1 CONNECTING AT THE HEART FOR COUPLES – The perfect CD for creating more love and intimacy with your partner! Julia leads couples through four separate exercises designed to nurture and connect.

PRICE: $15 plus $2 shipping and handling.

Order from: Julia Tindall
PO Box 601872
Sacramento CA 95860

For all inquiries call 916-486-4620 or e-mail yogajules@aol.com

ORDER FORM

Book		Qty	Total
20 Questions for Enlightened Living	$18.00	___	$________
Video Tapes			
A1 Standing Wave Yoga Floor Series	$25.00	___	$________
A2 Hatha Yoga Animal Series	$25.00	___	$________
A3 Partner Yoga	$25.00	___	$________
A4 Beginners' T'ai Chi	$25.00	___	$________
A5 Swedish Massage	$25.00	___	$________
B1 Shoulder Opening Series	$15.00	___	$________
B2 Dog and Pigeon Series	$15.00	___	$________
B3 Sun Salutation Set	$15.00	___	$________
B4 Seated Straddle, Camel and Lotus	$15.00	___	$________
B5 Seated Series	$15.00	___	$________
B6 Standing Straddle and Psoas	$15.00	___	$________
B7 Frog and Cobra Series	$15.00	___	$________
B8 Yoga for the Abs	$15.00	___	$________
Audiocassettes			
C1 Standing Wave Yoga Prone Series	$10.00	___	$________
C2 Animal Series Yoga	$10.00	___	$________
C3 Beginners' Yoga	$10.00	___	$________
C4 Creative Visualization	$10.00	___	$________
CD for Couples			
D1 Connecting at the Heart	$15.00	___	$________

SUBTOTAL $________

SALES TAX (CA residents only) $________

SHIPPING and HANDLING
U.S. – Books and Videotapes $3 each,
Audiocassettes $1 each,
CD's $2 each,
$9 maximum
Foreign – Call or email for rates $________

GRAND TOTAL
U.S. Dollars only. No foreign checks, please. $________

SHIPPING INFORMATION

First Name: ______________________________

Middle Initial: ___

Last Name: ______________________________

Address: ______________________________

____

____

Country: ______________________________

Phone: ______________________________

E-mail: ______________________________

_Visa _MasterCard

Credit Card #: ______________________________

Expiration Date: ________ Order Amount: $________

Signature: ______________________________

Mail this form with your check, money order, or credit card information to:

Julia Tindall
PO Box 601872
Sacramento CA 95860
USA

ORDER FORM

Book		Qty	Total
20 Questions for Enlightened Living	$18.00	___	$________
Video Tapes			
A1 Standing Wave Yoga Floor Series	$25.00	___	$________
A2 Hatha Yoga Animal Series	$25.00	___	$________
A3 Partner Yoga	$25.00	___	$________
A4 Beginners' T'ai Chi	$25.00	___	$________
A5 Swedish Massage	$25.00	___	$________
B1 Shoulder Opening Series	$15.00	___	$________
B2 Dog and Pigeon Series	$15.00	___	$________
B3 Sun Salutation Set	$15.00	___	$________
B4 Seated Straddle, Camel and Lotus	$15.00	___	$________
B5 Seated Series	$15.00	___	$________
B6 Standing Straddle and Psoas	$15.00	___	$________
B7 Frog and Cobra Series	$15.00	___	$________
B8 Yoga for the Abs	$15.00	___	$________
Audiocassettes			
C1 Standing Wave Yoga Prone Series	$10.00	___	$________
C2 Animal Series Yoga	$10.00	___	$________
C3 Beginners' Yoga	$10.00	___	$________
C4 Creative Visualization	$10.00	___	$________
CD for Couples			
D1 Connecting at the Heart	$15.00	___	$________

SUBTOTAL $________

SALES TAX (CA residents only) $________

SHIPPING and HANDLING
U.S. – Books and Videotapes $3 each,
Audiocassettes $1 each,
CD's $2 each,
$9 maximum
Foreign – Call or email for rates $________

GRAND TOTAL
U.S. Dollars only. No foreign checks, please. $________

SHIPPING INFORMATION

First Name: ______________________________

Middle Initial: ___

Last Name: ______________________________

Address: ______________________________

____

____

Country: ______________________________

Phone: ______________________________

E-mail: ______________________________

_Visa _MasterCard

Credit Card #: ______________________________

Expiration Date: ________ Order Amount: $________

Signature: ______________________________

Mail this form with your check, money order, or credit card information to:

Julia Tindall
PO Box 601872
Sacramento CA 95860
USA

Transformational Seminars based on *20 Questions for Enlightened Living*

Intensive seminars designed to empower the student in the practice of Self-inquiry. Discover hidden patterns from the unconscious that are blocking your true potential, practice activating the witness, release old belief systems that no longer serve and experience the love that arises when all else dissolves. These unique and powerful intensives will help you gain insight, clarity, and a fresh approach to life. One weekend can change your world forever! Practical, hands-on processes will be used based on the 20 Questions.

Weekend Retreats

Julia leads weekend retreats in the USA at healing sanctuaries such as Harbin Hot Springs, Sierra Hot Springs, and Mount Shasta. The weekends are yoga intensives where the student can immerse in the various yogic practices of hatha, jnana, bhakti yogas and meditation. With the support of Julia and the group, a loving energy is created that holds a safe and sacred space for transformation.

"I am still so high from the weekend! This is the best group of people I have ever attended a workshop with!" —Andy Andersen, Cochoran, CA

"I woke up on Monday morning after the Harbin weekend feeling as if the world had made the sweetest, purest love to me and I am eternally grateful!" —Lynn-Marie Murphy, Palo Alto, CA

"I want to thank you for the wonderful weekend at Harbin. You are so good at what you do! You have the voice and face of an angel and you were my guiding angel through the weekend. I felt so held and nurtured by you. One of my favorite moments was when you sang us a song while we were in meditation. Your soft, loving teaching style is exactly what I needed in my life and in my yoga right now!"—Alison Eby, Santa Rosa, CA

Call 916-486-4620 or e-mail yogajules@aol.com for upcoming seminar locations and dates, or visit www.juliatindall.com

Yoga Vacations

Julia regularly leads yoga vacations to Maya Tulum in Mexico, Bali, Costa Rica and Hawaii. The trips are characterized by a sense of openness, camaraderie, and free-flow in the spirit of "lila yoga," the yoga of play. Julia leads morning yoga sessions and sometimes evening sessions too. Participants are free to enjoy the local culture in between times.

"I can't begin to thank you for such a wonderful trip. I have never felt so alive and well. The yoga was life-altering and for the first time, I felt so much bliss, love and peace. I will take your love, your lessons of yoga and think often of my new family I met in Bali!" —Marie Exline, Burlingame, CA

"The first time I met Julia was when I was at a retreat center in Mexico where she was teaching yoga. I noticed her group was having so much fun—they all looked so radiant! So I asked if I could join them. With characteristic generosity Julia said yes. I have been joining her yoga vacations ever since. I love the people she attracts and the way the yoga helps me expand myself, both physically and spiritually." —Wheaton Griffin, Alabama

"If you don't have a great time on Julia's trips it's your own fault!" —Pat Nielsen, Carmichael, CA

"I have been on many of Julia's trips over the years and love the combination of adventure, great yoga and interesting people!" —Doug Scott, Sacramento, CA

Call 916-486-4620 or e-mail yogajules@aol.com for upcoming yoga vacations, or visit www.juliatindall.com